The European Reformation
A student's guide to the key ideas and the events they shaped

Studymates

25 Key Topics in Business Studies
25 Key Topics in Human Resources
25 Key Topics in Marketing
Accident & Emergency Nursing
Constitutional & Administrative Law
Cultural Studies
English Legal System
European Reformation
GCSE Chemistry
GCSE English
GCSE History: Schools History Project
GCSE Maths
GCSE Sciences
Genetics
Geology for Civil Engineers
Hitler & Nazi Germany
Land Law
Law of Evidence
Maths for Engineers
Memory
Organic Chemistry
Practical Drama & Theatre Arts
Revolutionary Conflicts
Science for Engineers
Sex, Memory & Psychology
Social Anthropology
Social Statistics
Speaking English
Speaking Better French
Studying Chaucer
Studying History
Studying Literature
Studying Poetry
Studying Psychology
Tourism Studies
Understanding Maths
Using Information Technology

Many other titles in preparation

Studymates

The European Reformation

A student's guide to the key ideas and the events they shaped

Andrew A. Chibi PhD

Lecturer in European History

Studymates

© Copyright 1999 by Andrew Chibi

First published in 1999 by Studymates, a Division of International Briefings Ltd, Plymbridge House, Estover Road, Plymouth PL6 7PY, United Kingdom.
Tel: (01752) 202301. Fax: (01752) 202333

Web site: http://www.studymates.co.uk
Customer services   email: cservs@plymbridge.com
Editorial email: editor@studymates.co.uk

All rights reserved. No part of this work may be reproduced or stored in an information retrieval system without the express permission of the Publishers given in writing.

Note: The contents of this book are offered for the purposes of general guidance only and no liability can be accepted for any loss or expense incurred as a result of relying in particular circumstances on statements made in this book. Readers are advised to check the current position with the appropriate authorities before entering into personal arrangements.

Case studies in this book are entirely fictional and any resemblance to real persons or organisations is entirely coincidental.

Produced for Studymates by Deer Park Productions.

Typeset by PDQ Typesetting, Newcastle-under-Lyme

Printed and bound by The Cromwell Press Ltd, Trowbridge, Wiltshire.

Contents

Foreword by Mark Greengrass		7
Author's Preface		8
Introduction		**9**
	One minute summary	9
	Why the reformation is important	9
	Reform under different formats	11
1	**Pre-reformation cultural factors**	**13**
	One minute summary	13
	The Renaissance	13
	The significance of the Western Schism	16
	Piety and the rising lay expectations	18
	Erasmus, humanism and 'Christian humanism'	20
	Tutorial	23
2	**Pre-reformation intellectual factors**	**25**
	One minute summary	25
	The structure of the church	25
	The theology of salvation	28
	The importance of the sacraments	31
	The pre-reformation use of scripture and tradition	33
	How to assess medieval heretical movements	34
	Tutorial	36
3	**Martin Luther**	**38**
	One minute summary	38
	Luther's *Ninety-Five Theses*	38
	Why Luther rejected other traditional religious ideas	42
	Luther's understanding of the sacraments	43
	The doctrine of *sola scriptura*	46
	The meaning of the 'priesthood of all believers'	48
	Why Luther rejected traditional salvation doctrine	49
	Luther's doctrine of 'justification by faith alone'	51
	The impact of Luther	52
	Tutorial	53
4	**The urban reformers**	**55**
	One minute summary	55
	The social and political context	55

The European Reformation

	The reformers and their cities	57
	Theological contrasts	59
	The urban reform programmes	63
	Tutorial	65
5	**Radical reformation**	**67**
	One minute summary	67
	Why the Anabaptists are important but obscure	67
	The radicals' key ideas	69
	The importance of Thomas Müntzer	72
	The importance of the city of Münster	73
	Tutorial	74
6	**Karlstadt**	**76**
	One minute summary	76
	Karlstadt: an obscure but key figure	76
	The concept of proto-Puritanism	77
	Karlstadt's theologies contrasted with Luther's	78
	Karlstadt, Müntzer and the Peasants' War	82
	Tutorial	83
7	**John Calvin**	**85**
	One minute summary	85
	Calvin and the second wave of the reformation	85
	Double predestination	87
	Calvin's theology of salvation	89
	Calvin's doctrine of the sacraments	91
	The church 'visible'	92
	The impact of Calvinism	94
	Tutorial	95
8	**The Catholic reformation**	**97**
	One minute summary	97
	Pre-Lutheran Catholic reform movements	97
	Papal reform	101
	The Council of Trent	104
	Tutorial	109
Conclusion		**111**
	One minute summary	111
	The impact of the European reformation	111
	The importance of the Thirty Years' War	115
Key dates		117
Glossary		119
Sources		124
Web sites for reformation studies		128
European Reformation syllabuses		138
Index		142

Foreword

Tests, exercises, assignment, appraisal – they are a fundamental and growing part of our lives, and not merely our student lives. As our world becomes more complex, we are required to be good at two things at one and the same time. We have to be capable specialists and in a number of different specialisms. And we are also required to be generalists – comprehensively informed about trends and developments more generally. Studymates answer these various needs. In this text, Andrew Chibi provides a reliable and effectively laid-out guide to prepare students for examinations on the European Reformation. He takes students and tutors alike to areas of more specialised debate in the subject, and summarises the issues without over-simplifying them. He provides an overview of a subject, the European Reformation, that fundamentally changed Europe. We are still living with the consequences of those changes.

Mark Greengrass
Professor of History
Sheffield University

Author's Preface

Although writing, of any kind, seems to be a very solitary pursuit, the number of intellectual debts which accumulate by the end are amazing. This is especially so for this kind of academic textbook. Many of the debts owed are to former students who asked the right questions at the right time and forced me to think about the answers. Although their actual names might now escape me, they attended my lectures, seminars and tutorials at Southampton, Manchester Metropolitan and Leicester Universities. Of course, I also bounced ideas off colleagues and friends who showed great tolerance in listening. So I would like to thank Andrew Pettegree and Mark Greengrass for inspiration, advice and support; Terry Hartley, Peter Musgrave and George Bernard for sound guidance; and Ian Campbell for his advice and belief in the project. I would also like to thank Ian, Dave, Paul, James, Andrew, Jo and Daz for keeping me slightly off balance throughout.

My greatest debts are to my family. To my wife Ellen, for her unwavering support, stimulation, encouragement, diversion and ideas; to my parents Andy and Eleanor, and in-laws George and Anne, my sisters Joan and Melinda, brothers Chris and Kevin, nieces Rachel and Marley, nephews Andrew, Christopher and Nicky. I would also like to thank John and Irene for their support and, lastly, I should mention Jake (who would squawk if I did not mention him) and my cousin Sadie (who might have done likewise).

Although these people can take some credit for the appearance of this book, all mistakes, gaffes, errors and evidence of poor scholarship are entirely my own.

Andrew Allan Chibi

Introduction

One minute summary – The term 'reformation' refers to the religious transformation of Europe in the sixteenth century. It was a movement of two parts. An expression of religious discontent was followed up by a working out of both local and national solutions. Many aspects of the powerful Roman Catholic Church, such as its doctrine and ceremonies, came into question and underwent sometimes drastic change. But, while discontent was common, the solutions were not. In fact, we can distinguish at least four equal, simultaneous 'types' – Lutheran, Reformed (or Calvinist), radical and Catholic (or Counter), each with contrasting local expressions. This introduction will help you to understand:

▶ why the reformation is important
▶ why the reformation needs to be studied
▶ how to recognise and contrast different 'types' and 'formats' of reformation.

Why the reformation is important

To many historians, the reformation marked the transition between medieval and modern cultures. Examining the period helps us understand the social structures, political methods and cultural developments existing in Europe (and much of the Western world) today. Understanding the reformation helps us to understand, for example, modern Christian fundamentalist movements, the attraction of cults, modern philosophy and, to a degree, the American or French Revolutions. In the sixteenth century, every aspect of life came into flux and the changes are with us still.

Why the sixteenth century was a period of flux
Two causes are basic:

1. recognition of the need for change
2. search for the best way to implement change.

There was widespread agreement that the church must be reformed. Abuses ought to be eliminated, popes must become more spiritual, the clergy better educated. After all, the church then was central to all aspects of life.

This reform was to be done by trying to recapture the vitality and freshness of the earlier Christian faith, as found in the golden age of its first centuries. The problem was in how to do this. The search accounts for the different types of reform. Some people looked to the moral reform of the papacy and a cleansing of its traditions. Others looked to a re-examination of New Testament documents. Others still wanted a complete reform of dogma, theology and other basic religious notions, or a reclamation of the original ideas. The reformation was, in many ways therefore, more a conservative, reactionary movement and less the radical revolutionary movement it is so often seen to be.

Who had the power to bring about reform?
This is an important question. By the early sixteenth century, a basic shift in power within Europe had been completed. Studying the reformation helps us to explain this shift. Papal authority had greatly diminished, while the power of secular governments had increased. In 1478, for instance, the Spanish Inquisition was established with power over the clergy, religious orders and church court system, but as an appendage of the crown, not the pope.

Throughout much of early modern Europe the power of the pope to impose reformation had been likewise steadily diminished, even had the will to reform been present. Oddly, there was no corresponding decrease in the power of local or national churches, only in ultimate leadership. Studying the reformation helps us explain this, too.

Reform under different formats

Given the shifting power structures, it is important to understand how and why reformers allied themselves with national, regional or civic powers. You will note that reform was often preceded by a symbiotic alliance of reformer and civic authority, each believing that reform was to their benefit. This arrangement also accounts for the sometimes bewildering variety of religious expressions evident in Western society today.

Historians have developed a number of terms to describe these various alliances, and it would be useful to distinguish them for later reference. The most common descriptions are these:

(a) mainstream – referring to the familiar, varied and non-radical movements of such figures as Luther and Calvin

(b) magisterial – referring to the manner in which the mainstream reformers called upon secular authorities (like city councils) to effect change

(c) radical – referring to the less familiar, more theologically fragmented and often more violent (and short-term) movements

(d) urban – referring to specifically and uniquely local movements influenced by humanism

(e) Counter – referring to the backlash movement of the Roman Catholics against the Protestants

(f) Protestant – referring to the undifferentiated collection of non-Catholic movements.

While all of these groupings are significant, the urban movement is of greatest consequence because of the central importance of cities in the period.

By the early sixteenth century, the councils of many cities had managed to gain, regain or sustain a substantial degree of autonomy. In effect, therefore, each city regarded itself as a miniature state (council = government and inhabitant = subject). Indeed, in fifty of the sixty-five imperial cities, in Switzerland and in France, reform also originated in urban contexts. Moreover, the success or failure of the various reformation movements depended largely upon the political and social factors present in the cities at the time. Cities also witnessed, first-hand, growing social unrest, as demands for broader-based and more representative governments gained momentum.

Thus, reformation became linked with demands for social change. Religion came to offer a focal point for all other grievances, economic, social or political. Examining the reformation helps us, therefore, to understand the origins of the modern world itself.

1

Pre-Reformation Cultural Factors

One minute summary – The life-styles of early modern Europeans, their concerns and solutions, all help explain why the reformation happened. Because religion was at the centre of life, both questions and solutions were phrased in religious terms. And, as life was harsh and short, the questions most often asked revolved around death, salvation and the church. More and more often, comparisons to life in the so-called 'golden' age (whenever that was) were being made, and Europeans of the late-medieval period found their own time wanting. Naturally, blame was cast at, and solutions were demanded from, the church. Solutions were not, however, often forthcoming. This chapter will help you to understand:

▶ the Renaissance and its importance
▶ the Western Schism, conciliarism, anti-clericalism and anti-papalism
▶ how to make sense of 'piety' and the rising expectations of the laity
▶ the significance of Erasmus, humanism and 'Christian' humanism.

The Renaissance

What is sure about the Renaissance is that the word is French for 'rebirth'. It indicates the period before the sixteenth century that witnessed the revival of the arts and classical studies in Italy and, subsequently, in the rest of Europe (*c.*1300–1600). Whether there was a re-awakening of civilisation after a long 'dark' age is less certain. There were changes, including:

▶ a new intellectual appreciation for personal experience

- the founding of universities
- a search for truth in nature
- greater value applied to direct observation.

By this period, religious orthodoxy had been settled, changeable only in minor aspects, including:

1. the doctrine of the Trinity (God as one substance of three persons – Father, Son and Holy Spirit)

2. God's omnipotence and omnipresence

3. that Jesus was both God and man, was crucified and was resurrected

4. original sin.

While all this agreement sounds good, it was this stability that led to stagnation.

Understanding the causes of stagnation

Religious stability eventually gave way to **scholasticism**, an intellectual method by which logical deduction was applied to the words, rather than the conclusions, of recognised authorities. The schoolmen deduced refinements, engaged in endless debates on pointless questions and made ever more narrow distinctions, rather than innovate. 'How many angels *can* dance on the head of a pin?' These debates distracted scholars and religious authorities from, nor could the collected data be applied to, real life problems.

The Renaissance might well have seen a 'flowering of the arts', but more serious problems were left unconsidered. The fourteenth and fifteenth centuries also witnessed a general tapering off of economic expansion. This resulted in many further problems, including:

- severe economic depression in the towns
- a decline in population
- a decline in cultivation

Pre-Reformation Cultural Factors

- a reduction in the volume of trade
- the decline in power of central authorities
- a withering of strong political figures
- increased warfare.

To understand why this stagnation occurred, we have to look to two events:

1. the Mongol invasions
2. the Black Death.

As a result of the first, the Holy Roman Empire was reduced to a rump authority out of which independent states and cities were carved (highlighting nationalism). These towns were themselves also visited upon with mass destruction. Thus, the usual sources of the cultural, intellectual and craft movements were devastated. The Black Death further reduced populations. On the positive side, people, materials and new ideas flooded into Italy from worse hit eastern lands.

Alien and distinctive cultural ideas were introduced into Europe, and new political, legal and artistic notions were experienced. The clash between older and newer ideas, however, led to reactions against spiritual or intellectual authorities (who had ignored the problems), and to a search for fresh spiritual forms. The upshot is that, although established theologies were retained on the basic doctrinal level, new advances to God were being made in either new forms of intellectual expression (like humanism) or by vigorous anti-authoritarian criticisms (like anti-clericalism or anti-papalism).

- *You are there* – Imagine yourself living in medieval Europe. Your family has been devastated by the Black Death, your livelihood destroyed by economic depression and your very life itself threatened by seemingly endless military actions. You would turn to the church for help and guidance, but they seem more interested in pursuing endless debate. How do you feel about this? Would you begin to look elsewhere for spiritual succour?

One truism of history is that heightened intellectual activity often produces rival personal and spiritual movements (see below). If this were not enough, the central religious authorities failed to recognise the dangers, trapped as they were in their own problems.

The significance of the Western Schism

Conciliarism, anti-clericalism and anti-papalism
The Renaissance left many people confused and morally unsure. People felt insecure, and life seemed unstable at best. Another crisis grew out of the fact that the church, the supposed fountainhead of stability, was itself obviously unstable.

Understanding the causes of instability
A real problem existed between the power claimed by the pope and how much of it Western European rulers were prepared to recognise. The origin of this dilemma is the so-called Donation of Constantine (the emperor's endowment of church lands and granting of political authority to the papacy). The papacy claimed the right, based on the Donation, to crown (or depose) the Western emperor himself. When the empire declined, how much power did the popes have over the rulers of the small, independent kingdoms carved out of it? The answer was worked out over the intervening centuries. For example:

(a) The 'Investiture Contest' of 1075 established a church free of lay interference (no layman could invest a clergyman with clerical office).

(b) Pope Urban II used the Crusades as a political platform and established himself as the moral voice of Christian Europe, and as its diplomatic focus.

(c) Pope Innocent III adopted the title 'vicar of Christ', in theory, subordinating all other authorities.

(d) The fourth Lateran Council of 1215 reinforced clerical immunity to civil laws.

Pre-Reformation Cultural Factors

There were signs, however, that the church was pushing too far:

1. Thomas à Kempis and the Brethren of the Common Life established lay religious orders, side-stepping clerical authority.

2. Pope Boniface VIII (*c*.1235–1303) tried to induce clerical immunity to taxation (this failed) and issued *Unam Sanctum* (1302). This embodied the principle of supreme papal authority over both spiritual and temporal matters (the famous last straw)

In 1303, Boniface was kidnapped by French forces and held prisoner while King Philip (the Fair) procured the election of a French bishop as Pope Clement V (1305). He, in turn, moved the seat of authority from Rome to Avignon. This initiated the so-called seventy-years long 'Babylonish captivity of the papacy' and the Western Schism. As a result, several problems developed, including:

(a) The opulence of the Avignon popes, at a time of severe economic depression, offended both clergy and laity alike.

(b) Increased clerical taxation gave rise to anti-papalism (among priests) and anti-clericalism (among the laity).

(c) The cardinals' attempted move back to Rome in 1377 split the church, each side electing its own pope and each claiming legitimacy (in 1409 an ecumenical council at Pisa was summoned, proclaimed both popes deposed and proceeded to elect a third!).

Thus, the ludicrous situation emerged wherein the fountainhead of all stability was itself split into three warring factions. Although that problem was resolved (the council of Constance, 1414–18, named one legitimate pope, Martin V), it was too late to halt the impression of a corrupt church hierarchy.

Understanding conciliarism

▶ *You are there* – Imagine yourself living through the 'schism' period. Whereas inflated papal claims and obstinacy had given rise to three rival popes, a general council had solved the problem in a stroke. Would you rather see more general councils or a return to unrestricted papal power?

As a general council had succeeded where various popes had failed, the conciliarist theory developed. Conciliarists thought that general councils should be accorded the highest spiritual authority (even over the popes) and should be summoned regularly to deal with problems. Although Martin V agreed, subsequent popes viewed conciliarism as a dangerous challenge (rather than as an aid) to their own authority. In fact, up to the 1800s, only one general council (Trent, 1545–63) was summoned. Crisis averted, the papacy reverted to its worldly, Italio-centric outlook, giving further rise to anti-papalism and anti-clericalism (expressed in oral, literary and physical criticisms). The cry most often heard was, when will the church be reformed?

Piety and the rising lay expectations

Oddly, despite the problems, by the fifteenth century lay piety was stronger than ever before. As people could not rely on the authorities for spiritual succour, they looked elsewhere (and inward). The Mass grew in popularity, as did religious endowments, and the membership of both religious and lay brotherhoods also grew (lay movements concentrated on inner contemplation and meditations, but enforced no religious vows). Increasingly, devotion and popular piety also gave rise to increased demand for religious literature and the open expression of discontent with clerical abuses, the motives of Italio-centric popes and the very condition of the priesthood itself. Other hallmarks of popular piety included:

(a) the rise in pilgrimages
(b) increased buying and selling of indulgences
(c) the doctrine of purgatory (see below).

This rising level of devotion in Christian Europe, however, shrouded

Pre-Reformation Cultural Factors

a number of serious problems:

1. The cult of saints gave rise to fraudulence in the trading of relics.
2. The increased demand for relics bordered on idolatry.
3. Reliance on saintly intercession and the cult of Mary seemed to make the clergy redundant.
4. Religion turned less spiritual and more material oriented.
5. Indulgences and purgatory made religious faith financially burdensome.

By the sixteenth century, or so it seemed, salvation (getting to heaven) was no longer a matter of faith alone but a combination of faith and good works which had, in effect, reduced it to a gamble.

▶ *You are there* – Imagine yourself living at the time and wondering where security and salvation were to be found. Religious authorities (untrustworthy) struggled hard to spread the doctrine that man was justified by faith in God's grace, but the dual disasters of the fourteenth century, and the resulting rise in popular piety, meant that people sought security for themselves and for their loved ones elsewhere. Would you have looked elsewhere?

Anyway, more monasteries were founded in order to guarantee that prayers for the souls of the founder and his family were said in perpetuity, and indulgences were developed so that people could buy their way out of time in purgatory. The belief developed (and priests did not disabuse people of it) that people could earn their way into heaven by their own labours.

In brief, a man needed a certain amount of grace (as if it were some kind of heavenly currency) to get into heaven (how much was unknown). Through his good works and acts of charity he built up a grace account for himself or his loved ones (how much he had built up at any time was unknown). By believing in Jesus, the scriptures, church traditions and so on, he would merit grace, but never enough to get into heaven immediately after his death. His soul went, instead, to purgatory (for how long was unknown). Salvation also came to depend (to a degree) on the sacrament of penance (examined in Chapter 2). For all of this, salvation was still never a certainty.

Erasmus, humanism and 'Christian humanism'

As we have seen, medieval scholarship was dominated by the so-called 'scholastics', of which there are two types:

1. the realists of Aquinas (ascendant up to $c.1350$)
2. the nominalists of William of Ockham (ascendant thereafter to $c.1500$). For our purposes, the two sub-types of nominalism are important. These are:

    (a) the modern way (*via moderna*)
    (b) the modern Augustinian school (*schola Augustiniana moderna*).

The main dispute here centred on the perennial question of man's contribution to, or the human element in, salvation.

The moderns took a positive, optimistic view that man did contribute to his own salvation (in obviously quite small ways). The Augustinians took a more negative, pessimistic view that man contributed nothing, God alone justifies. The split left scholasticism open to further intellectual challenge in the fifteenth century, the most important of which was 'humanism'.

In brief, humanism resulted from a renewed interest in the writings of antiquity, but not necessarily on religious grounds. Rather, scholars looked at Greek and Latin texts, in and of themselves, in terms of language, grammar and literary styles, inspiring a new appreciation for all original sources. Most importantly, the humanists focused attention on human potential rather than on divine mysteries. By the fifteenth century, humanism had given rise to a new appreciation of the accomplishments of antiquity (like Platonic logic) which had been smothered by medieval religious superstitions.

Pre-Reformation Cultural Factors

From its origins in fourteenth-century Italy, humanism spread north via trade, the exchange of diplomats and wandering scholars. Almost by necessity, the new methods took on regional variations (like Ximenes in Spain or d'Etaples in France), which gave rise to two obvious, distinct and defining differences:

1. Christian humanism
2. secular humanism.

The former – key for us – bypassed scholasticism in an effort to examine Platonic ideas in their original forms, while retaining an orthodox religious tone. Humanist scholars encouraged a clear, less scholastic understanding of the basic aspects of faith. They opined that by developing the gifts God had giving man, man could strive to find God.

The detailed study of the original texts also gave rise, in Northern Europe especially, to an equally detailed examination of scripture as the foundation of a new harmonisation of faith and reason. While Northern Europeans explored this religious type, Italians explored the second, secular type (sometimes called 'civic humanism') and found that active involvement in civic affairs was increasingly worthwhile. The involvement of scholars in government, bureaucracy and trade not only enhanced human potential, but also brought about other changes, including:

(a) the study of history as a unique discipline separate from theology
(b) the study of politics as a discipline in its own right.

Erasmus
Of the Christian humanist scholars, Desiderius Erasmus (c.1466–1536) was probably the most important.

Erasmus had two objectives for his scholarship – to discredit scholastic theology and to reduce popular superstition – thinking he could encourage a more practical Christianity, thereby, one suitable for both clergy and laity. His method included:

(a) an attack on the abuse of outward forms of religious devotion

(b) criticism of the cult of saints

(c) encouragement for reading of the Bible and Church Fathers in their original languages, avoiding glosses and commentaries.

The end product was his *Greek New Testament* (1516), which focused attention on translation errors in the standard Latin *Vulgate*. Of course, highlighting errors in the church's official version of scripture, criticising the spiritual life and raising other questions also further encouraged anti-papalism and anti-clericalism.

Understanding the impact of cultural changes

Combining anti-papalism and anti-clericalism with the growth of literacy and late medieval lay piety produced an explosive situation, the most obvious and immediate expression of which was the rise in heresies, such as Lollardy (in England), the Hussites (in Bohemia) or the Waldenses (in Savoy-Piedmont). All three were, more or less, nationalistic movements focusing on the needs of their own people above the needs of a seemingly narrowly Italian-based church. Although not necessarily 'anti-church', they merely raised doubts about the papacy –

▶ its 'foreign' nature

▶ its seemingly money-based doctrines

▶ its sacramental system

– and much else besides. Moreover, they emphasised secular control of clerical institutions and wanted copies of vernacular scriptures produced so that they could be read and fully understood by every single believer. These same beliefs would, for the most part, be reflected by the major thinkers of the sixteenth century. For example:

(a) Machiavelli called for the reform of the church's moral, legal and administrative systems (and wanted a properly educated clergy).

(b) Erasmus questioned the spirituality of the church, hoping to recapture its earlier vitality.

(c) Luther demanded a reformation of Christian doctrine altogether.

Reformation in early modern Christian Europe was, therefore, pursued in a number of ways, in all of which the same elements appear for re-examination, including:

- papal authority
- scripture and tradition
- the sacramental system
- the distinctions between priests and laymen.

In the sixteenth century, the concentration on these issues (and some others) split the western church into two irreconcilable groups, Protestants and 'Roman' Catholics.

Tutorial

Summary of key ideas
(The) Renaissance – the period (*c.*1300–1600) in which art and learning was revived under the influence of classical models. Beginning in Italy, it spread north to the rest of Europe in the fifteenth century.

(The) Western Schism – the seventy-year period sometimes called the 'Babylonish captivity of the papacy', during which there were two, and then three, simultaneous popes.

Conciliarism – the theory that general councils (not popes) should be the ultimate authority on religious matters.

Anti-clericalism – opposition to the power of the clergy, particularly in secular matters.

Anti-papalism – opposition to the power of the papacy, particularly in secular matters.

Piety – personal devotion or intense intrinsic religious feeling.

Humanism – a way of thinking which emphasises the individual.

Progress questions
1. Why was salvation considered a gamble?

2. How did humanism inspire religious reformation?

Seminar discussion
1. Which factor caused more anti-church sentiment – humanism or internal (self-imposed) problems in the church itself?

2. How did the cultural changes of the Renaissance period inspire religious change?

Practical assignment
Imagine yourself as a wandering scholar. Write a letter back to your mentors outlining the differences between humanism north and south of the Alps and what implications these might have for religion.

Study and revision tips
1. Create a simple chronological chart to help you visualise the important cultural events.

2. Create a chart of two columns with cultural events listed in one and related religious reactions in the other.

2

Pre-Reformation Intellectual Factors

One minute summary – The reformation was not a single, consolidated movement. It was a series of individual actions inspired by a perceived need for change, inspiring both dogmatic and doctrinal changes. The call for change was neither widespread nor grassroots; people were generally content with the church's teachings. It was the abuse of those teachings (theology, dogma) and aspects of its structure and organisation (hierarchy) which were resented. This chapter will help you to understand:

- the structure of the church
- the theory of human salvation
- the importance of the seven sacraments
- the pre-reformation use of scripture and tradition
- how to assess important heretical movements.

The structure of the church

In the period under examination the church regulated European society, much as royal governments regulated kingdoms. At the national level, archbishops and bishops influenced government while, at the parish level, the priest was the dominant figure in the community. The religious, social, political and economic ideas of the church were the ideas practised by, and enforced upon, the people. People were, generally, happy with this.

Understanding the church hierarchy
On earth, the head of the church, ultimate judge, legislator, and doctrinal and biblical interpreter was the pope, but all was not well and authority was abused. The popes were increasingly less spiritual and more political minded. Indeed, when Leo X was elected pope

(1513), he said: 'Now that God has given us the papacy, let us enjoy it' (Lindberg, p.55). There were checks and balances on papal authority, including the *curia* and the general council (examined above), but these were weak.

The *curia* was the Roman civil service. It was staffed by cardinals (nominally independent but appointed by popes), responsible to elect new popes. Outside Rome, by the sixteenth century, the papacy had been forced into a series of compromises with local rulers over the election of local clerical officers. The Concordat of Bologna, for example, negotiated between Francis I of France and Leo X (1516), provided the king with certain recommended practical qualifications to guide his selection of the higher clergy, leaving the pope a 'rubber stamping' role. These local officers were the bishops, archbishops, abbots, priors and their own sub-officers.

The bishops and archbishops were the highest secular clerical authorities and were often very powerful landowners, too. They provided the connection between court (holding governmental offices) and diocese. The parishes were controlled by priests who might themselves have lower officers still, such as vicars, curates, rectors and chaplains, all under the authority of the bishops, themselves under the authority of archbishops. The regular clergy – the monastic orders and wandering friars – were ruled over by abbots, who might also control extensive estates or hold government office, assisted by priors. Ordinary laymen had no voice in the running of the church. However, they could form their own religious groups, called confraternities, to perform collective acts of charity or live the spiritual life without taking religious vows.

One problem with the church hierarchy was the question of control. All levels, from pope to humble curate, knew the extent of their power, were jealous of their own authority and knew how to by-pass higher authority without too much trouble. Thus, the day-to-day working of the church defied logic.

Understanding the failings within the hierarchy

Modern students should be familiar with hierarchies (look at the government itself) and will know that uniform perfection is impossible. The medieval church structure suffered many familiar problems, including:

Pre-Reformation Intellectual Factors

- nepotism
- greed
- sexual incontinence (lack of self-restraint)
- absenteeism (leaving someone else in charge)
- pluralism (holding several offices)
- worldliness (pursuing the material rather than the spiritual).

But, as bad as these things were, it is easy to see how these conditions were practically unavoidable.

As in any hierarchy, once a position is attained its powers have to be consolidated. A bishop must secure his position (perhaps by promoting the interests of his own family or class) and, once secured, could initiate improvements in a number of ways, like:

(a) rebuilding (or repair) programmes
(b) holding visitations of the parishes (to enforce discipline)
(c) sponsoring scholars, etc.

It must be acknowledged that bishops owed their positions to the ruler who nominated them and to the pope who approved them so they, and other high ranking officers, had to balance service to God with service to the state, often resulting in absenteeism and uninspired religious regimes.

Moreover, there were no hard and fast rules. The secular clergy was composed of rich and worldly cathedral deans (often pluralists) and poor rural curates (earning a meagre wage) alike, while the regular clergy might inhabit rich or poor monasteries. Although it was nominally within the bishop's powers to control these appointments, and thus oversee the character of the clergy in his diocese, ordination ceremonies could be attended elsewhere out of one bishop's control. As a result, necessary qualifications such as age, legitimacy and morals could be by-passed. Moreover, special papal grants of immunity from episcopal interference could also be bought. The result? – in one case, an eight-year-old bishop! A parish priest ignorant of the fundamentals of Christianity might slip through the net, or that same priest might have a mistress and illegitimate children to support. Even this might be overlooked at the local level if it was not flaunted. Provided such things were not overly abused, people seemed content, but...

▶ *You are there* – Imagine yourself living in the parish of a reprehensible priest. Would you accept the leadership of a man who could not control his sexual appetites or his greed? Would you listen to him as he advises you to live humbly and moderately, while he lives like a prince? Would you, instead, call him a hypocrite and demand improvements?

The theology of salvation

In order to understand salvation, related issues of justification, grace, predestination and the sacraments, and how abuses were creeping in, it is necessary for the student to grasp its two central themes:

(a) its grounding in the life, death and resurrection of Jesus
(b) how it is modelled on Jesus himself.

Understanding the role of Jesus in salvation
The theology of salvation was linked to the life, death and resurrection of Jesus in one of two ways: either as the demonstration of a new idea (his sacrifice as the guarantee of saving grace) or as a demonstration of an existing, but ill-perceived, idea (the reconciliation between God and man). The debate – which still rages – was whether Jesus's troubles revealed something old or established something new.

Whichever is the case, salvation is also linked to Jesus as a model. In other words, his life is an example of the redeemed life, and it shows Christians how to live, either:

▶ in imitation – Jesus as example to live by
▶ *or* in complete renewal and regeneration – a 'rebirth' in faith.

Understanding 'justification'
The basic question of salvation is: what must a Christian do to get into heaven? The simple answer is that he must be righteous or free of the taint of sin. Simple enough, one might think, but there is a difficulty.

Pre-Reformation Intellectual Factors

Although man was created innocent and in the image of God, this changed with the sin of Adam. The sin was twofold – pride and faithlessness. Adam had eaten of the fruit of the tree of knowledge, thinking that he could become like God (pride), even though God have forbidden it (faithlessness, lack of trust and acceptance of God's promises). Afterwards, human nature became corrupt and humans become inclined toward sin of all kinds. Augustine, the most respected Church Father, understood this to mean that man was no longer the creature God had intended.

▶ *Picturing the scene* – You go to Church and confess your sins so that the priest will absolve you of the guilt through the grace of God and the saints. But, no matter how moral or how good you think yourself to be, no matter how often you confess or how many good works you do, you are still a sinner and still carry the taint of guilt for it. You might not have murdered anyone or stolen anything, you might be a paragon of virtue, but, simply by having been born, you are guilty of original sin by association.

Understanding the human element in salvation

Is there anything man can do? For Augustine, people could do nothing to change their sinfulness. It had become inherent in human nature; God had to step in, and did so through Jesus, to save humanity. This was divine saving 'grace'. Not everybody was saved, however. God had predestined some people for salvation, but not others. How this works is a mystery. There was an opposing point of view, however, which came to be known as **Pelagianism**.

Pelagius, a contemporary of Augustine, argued that man could earn salvation through the performance of good works and acts of charity. God gave 'fallen' man a chance: observe the Ten Commandments and live by the example of Jesus, and salvation could be merited. In the early days of the church, Pelagianism was adjudged heretical, as it seemed to deny the omnipotence of God. By the time of the scholastics and humanists, theorising had produced more arguments than solutions.

Recall how small kingdoms had been carved out of the once great Holy Roman Empire. To ensure stability, kings promised certain obligations to their people and vice versa. This was understood as an inherent 'political covenant' and it generally worked. Nominalist theologians began to look at religion in the same way – God had inherent obligations to his people and vice versa – a 'religious covenant'. The idea, at least, had the strength of Old Testament usage. The covenant established which duties had to be met to achieve salvation. Essentially, this meant trying to do good things and reject evil things. When realists asked how this was not simply Pelagianism restated, it was defended largely (and oddly) in economic terms:

▶ *Picturing the scene* – Consider a bank note. In and of itself it has little real value, since it is only a piece of paper. However, a government ascribes value to it in terms of pure silver or gold. The nominalists adapted this argument. Human works, although of little inherent value, have been (graciously) ascribed great value by God.

Understanding how abuse crept into the theory

Concepts of purgatory were appended to this because no one knew just how much grace was required to get into heaven, and so no one knew where the soul went upon death of the body. The theory developed that, when your body dies, your soul spends a certain amount of time – depending on how much guilt you still have – being punished (to purge the guilt) in purgatory. Abuse crept into these beliefs in that money became involved.

Purgatory was a frightening prospect. The very idea of a thousand, ten thousand or a million years of punishment was enough to unnerve anyone, particularly those who were unsure of salvation. Knowing that, no matter how much charity was given, good works performed or confessions made, they would never be enough often led to despair. However, by the medieval period the pope claimed that as God's agent on earth he had the power to grant grace, that is, alleviate guilt and reduce punishment time in exchange for 'special considerations'. This was known as the power of 'binding and loosening'.

These special considerations included such things as undertaking a pilgrimage to Jerusalem or other holy site, helping to build a church or going on a crusade against the infidel (in other words, *extra*-good works). Obviously, not everyone can go on a pilgrimage or a crusade so, to solve this dilemma, it was decided (*c*.1300s) that a money payment (buying an indulgence) was an acceptable alternative. For a certain amount you would get a receipt (a document) which meant that you were absolved of guilt, and thus of some punishments, as if you had gone on the pilgrimage or the crusade. Later, it was decided that souls already being punished in purgatory could also benefit from indulgences bought on their behalf.

While this seems compassionate, and even logical, of course some people were so frightened by the prospects that they might spend their entire life's savings on indulgences for their own benefit or for that of departed loved ones (a lost child?). We will come back to this.

The importance of the sacraments

The sacraments were church rites and ceremonies which had special spiritual qualities in that they each conveyed divine grace unto the recipient through the intervention of the priest. The priest performed the ritual and, thus, worked a miracle (consecration). There were seven sacraments:

1. **Baptism**, the rite of initiation into the church wherein a child is dipped into blessed water (to signify the death of Jesus) and then lifted out (to signify resurrection).

2. **Confirmation**, the rite of ratification of baptism.

3. The **eucharist**, the rite in which the priest offers the dedication, transforms the bread and wine into the body and blood of Jesus (**transubstantiation**) which, in essence, causes Jesus to suffer death once again for the benefit (**grace**) of the recipients.

4. **Extreme unction**, the last rite wherein the priest anoints the dying or terminally ill with unction (thereby granting grace).

5. **Matrimony**, an odd rite wherein the priest merely performs the ceremony while the couple enter into the state of grace for themselves.

6. **Ordination**, the rite by which a man becomes a priest through episcopal laying on of hands. This confirmed apostolic succession and conferred a special grace which could never be removed or lost.

7. **Penance**, the rite by which the individual repented the shame of his sins. Penance was composed of five elements:
    contrition (shame)
    confession (admission of sin)
    satisfaction (performing a chore to earn forgiveness)
    regeneration (change of life)
    absolution (the removal of the taint of sin by a priest)
all of which will become important later.

Understanding where abuses could occur

Abuses crept into the sacramental system in the medieval period in a number of ways. First, the doctrine of the sacraments came to illustrate the weaknesses inherent in scholastic theology. The sacraments had not been considered all that important in the early days of the church and, certainly, were not based exclusively on scriptural evidences. They came to be seen as medieval additions or man-made traditions.

Second, the sacraments seemed to represent the special power of the priesthood and, indeed, hidden knowledge. Priests, and only priests, performed the rites except in the odd case of matrimony and, usually, as the rites were performed in Latin (the liturgy), only the priests could fully understand it, in theory anyway. Thus, the sacraments and, therefore, participation in the church were something done on behalf of the congregation. The priests stood between God and man. The problem here was that the priests – if they were unscrupulous – could withhold grace from people they disliked or who were in their debt.

▶ *You are there* – Imagine yourself living in late medieval Europe. You know that if you do not receive absolution for your sins you will go to purgatory or even hell itself. What would you be willing to do to stay within the priests' good graces, knowing that even 'evil' priests could still legitimately perform the sacraments and grant grace?

The pre-reformation use of scripture and tradition

The Bible lies at the heart of Christianity but, in the conventional Catholic worship which had developed by the sixteenth century, it was of surprisingly little real importance when compared with the use of man-made traditions. Yes, a few passages were incorporated into the liturgy, but these were read in Latin, incomprehensible to the laymen and sometimes ill-understood by the priests themselves. But, as this was the way it had always been, people were content to participate in a passive way. The Bible would be explained to them, if and when necessary.

The importance of the Bible in the medieval period

It was important; it was considered, by the scholastic theologians, as the central and only relevant source of theology. The problem was that it was imprecise on many important matters. For example, at what point in the ceremony *does* the bread and wine become the body and blood? Moreover, some passages were obscure in meaning, while others seemed contradictory. Scholars and lawyers could only really guess at what these passages meant (hence debate). Collected together, these assumptions and guesses became the traditions.

As time progressed, the more popular traditions became **dogma** (the correct view). By the late-medieval period, it was the case that the Bible and the collected traditions could be separated and equally considered as sources of revelation. Moreover, as the Bible said nothing at all on a number of issues, unwritten or oral traditions from the time of the Apostles were also collected and given authority similar to the Bible and the written traditions. Obviously, just about anything could be justified by this conveniently unrecorded version of tradition. But, lest the student think the Bible had no importance, it was still considered the central source of theology and, as such, it was necessary to have a standard edition.

St Jerome, in the fifth century, drew up a common text of Latin translations which became the *Vulgate* or *textus vulgatus* – the standardised Latin version – in the thirteenth century. The rise of universities and theology departments in the Renaissance period made a standard *Vulgate* version imperative so that scholars and theologians had a common point of reference. It must be said, however, that the *Vulgate* was not a church-based venture. Rather, it was a business venture by the theologians and stationers of Paris and, like any business venture, the point was to make money and not necessarily to produce perfect texts.

Understanding the humanist impact

Progressing in time, however, we encounter those scholars who had been looking back toward the original literary and philosophical resource materials, the humanists. They valued and celebrated, above all else, the original source materials of the faith as well – Hebrew and Aramaic Old Testament and Greek New Testament writings – and began making comparisons between these sources and the *Vulgate*. What they found was shocking. They also valued the Greek language in particular, as the source of philosophy. As a consequence, New Testament studies and its importance began to seriously outweigh Old Testament studies and its importance to Christian theology. The humanist scholars became very important in bridging the gap between the ancient forms of religion and the reformers, who searched for a means of capturing the ancient forms.

The humanists were important because:

1. They provided the new literary tools (for example, Erasmus's *Greek New Testament* of 1516).

2. They developed textual analysis techniques, which uncovered textual errors.

3. They by-passed the need for explanatory texts and commentaries and made studies of the Bible more direct and personal for the theologians.

4. They argued for the development of a scripturally literate laity as the key to a rejuvenated Christianity.

How to assess medieval heretical movements

Finally, something needs to be said about the influence of medieval

Pre-Reformation Intellectual Factors

heresy movements. Basically, anyone who disagreed with the papacy was a heretic but, for our purposes, there are a few movements which need to be briefly examined. These are:

▶ Lollards (in England)
▶ Hussites (in Bohemia)
▶ Waldenses (in Savoy-Piedmont).

Understanding the importance of medieval heresy

As stated in Chapter 1, all three were nationalistic movements which focused on the needs of their own people, rather than on the needs of a largely foreign Roman Catholic hierarchy and Italian-based church.

Jan Hus and the Hussites
Jan Hus (*c*.1372–1415) was the inspiration behind the largest movement, the Hussites, a nearly national rebellion. A passionate preacher from Prague, Hus condemned the vices of his contemporaries. He led an academic movement against 'nominalist' scholasticism, and its near-Pelagian position on salvation, and followed Wyclif in doubting that sinful priests could validly perform the sacraments. After Hus was condemned and burnt in 1415, the Bohemian nobility revolted against Roman clerical authority, confiscated church lands and installed their own clerical officers. Moreover, they changed the Mass ceremony so that the laity was given the wine as well as the bread, and it became more centrally important as a focus for the community of the faithful. Luther will be accused of the 'Hussite heresy'.

John Wyclif and the Lollards
As mentioned, Wyclif influenced Hus on certain issues, but he was more important as a critic of the Roman claims to represent the true church. For Wyclif, the church was simply the community of the faithful. Although never burnt, Wyclif was exiled away from his Oxford University base. To carry on his reform efforts he turned to an emphasis on wandering preachers – who never taught at any one location for long but wrote up their sermons in manuscript form for wider distribution – and to English vernacular translations. His

followers, the Lollards, carried on into the reformation period:
1. denying the sacraments' transmission of grace
2. rejecting such traditions as images, pilgrimages and saint worship
3. encouraging group Bible-reading sessions.

Peter Valdes and the Waldenses
The Waldenses movement was originally influenced by Peter Valdes, an advocate of lay preaching. It was centred in southern France, northern Italy and parts of Germany. Although their actual 'heresy' is obscure, they were often charged as having rejected official church dogma and practices. Like the Lollards, they rejected sinful priests, purgatory and prayers for the souls of the dead. They also advocated wandering preachers and the spread of self-produced literature.

New alternatives
For our purposes, what is most significant about these movements are not their doctrines (important though these are) but the fact that they showed their sixteenth-century counterparts that it was possible to create a viable alternative to Roman Catholicism.

Tutorial

Summary of key ideas
Church hierarchy – the power structure of the Roman church consisting of the pope and cardinals (in Rome) at the top and archbishops, bishops and priests (in the European localities).

Salvation (or justification) – ascending to heaven after death, and the requirements which have to be met to do so.

Pelagianism – an ancient heresy which claimed that man can influence his own salvation through good works and acts of charity.

Indulgences – papal documents (receipts) issued in exchange for money payments made *in lieu* of performing a good work.

Pre-Reformation Intellectual Factors

Sacraments – church ceremonies performed to grant grace to the recipients.

Bible (scripture, the 'Word') – the collection of 'apostolic' or approved works which form the literary basis of the Christian religion.

Heresy – any expression or movement judged to be contrary to official church pronouncements on doctrine, dogma or canon law.

Progress questions
1. How did the scholastics come to develop three sources of revelation?

2. How did errors and abuses manage to creep into Catholicism in the pre-reformation period?

Seminar discussion
1. Why were people content to accept religion in such a passive manner?

2. What contribution did the humanists make to undermining Roman Catholic authority?

3. If you had been living at the time, how would the various heresy movements have made a difference in your own life?

Practical assignment
Imagine yourself as a wandering scholar. Write a letter back to your mentors outlining the differences between the scholastics and the humanists on religious issues of your choice.

Study and revision tips
1. Create a simple chronological chart to help you visualise the important intellectual factors discussed above.

2. Create a chart of four columns. List theological issues in the first, and the ancient, medieval and humanist understandings of them in the others.

3

Martin Luther

One minute summary – Martin Luther (1483–1546) was born at Eisleben in Saxony, and studied philosophy at Erfurt (1501–5). He joined the reformed Augustinians and taught theology at Wittenberg thereafter. Luther is significant because of the widespread acceptance of his challenge to the beliefs and traditions of Roman Catholicism. Although not the first to dissent, he was the first theologian to cause a permanent fracture in western Christendom. Because of him, doubts about traditional doctrines and practices had been introduced into the European consciousness. This chapter will help you to understand:

- the importance of Luther's *Ninety-Five Theses*
- why Luther rejected certain traditional religious ideas
- Luther's different understanding of the sacraments
- what Luther meant by *sola scriptura* and its wider significance
- what Luther meant by *the priesthood of all believers*
- why Luther rejected the traditional theory of human salvation
- how to make sense of the concept *justification by faith alone*.

Luther's Ninety-Five Theses

On 31st October 1517, Luther posted the *Ninety-Five Theses* to the castle church door in Wittenberg. This document was both a statement of ninety-five debatable propositions against the selling of indulgences, and an invitation to other scholars to join the debate – an early form of academic conference.

Understanding Luther's opposition to indulgences
We have discussed indulgences earlier (Chapter 2). Although they

might be seen as evidence of compassion on behalf of the pope, Luther had reasonable objections to them:

(a) As a theologian, he knew that God is omnipotent and omnipresent (so knew from the time of creation which individuals were saved or damned).

(b) Salvation was, therefore, God's free gift, which humans could not influence. Consequently Luther reckoned that, as humans could not influence salvation, those who bought indulgences were being tricked.

(c) As a proud German, Luther did not like his countrymen being fooled for the pope's financial gain.

The church's agent, the Dominican friar Johann Tetzel, was selling a unique indulgence in the Wittenberg area. This 'special issue' had the power to absolve from all sin or guarantee the immediate release from purgatory of the soul of a departed loved one. He even had an amusing sales pitch – '*As soon as the coin in the coffer rings, the soul from purgatory springs*' (Randell, p.24). Luther assumed that poor buyers were giving up all their possessions and money on a false hope, while the rich were buying *carte blanche* to sin without fear of punishments. He posted the *Theses* to draw attention to, and stop, this kind of nonsense.

Understanding Luther's arguments against indulgences

Luther's actual words are less important – you will never be asked to learn them – than his meaning. Luther believed indulgences to be useless, maybe even harmful, and wanted to convince others. But, by doing so, he was also attacking the very fundamentals of the Catholic faith and the very essence of Catholicism – good works and charity – upon which the entire structure of the church was based. This was controversial in at least three ways.

First, the church was a significant power broker in early modern Germany. Luther lived in a politically fragmented empire of small semi-independent states and cities under the nominal rule of an elected emperor. Seven regional rulers, known as 'electors', mighty in their own lands, also picked the emperors. Three of these seven, the archbishops of Mainz, Trier and Cologne, were clergymen, a sign of the exceptional political power of the church. It controlled vast territories and many of its prelates were also heads of state or 'prince-prelates', the fountainheads of political, social and economic power. Undermine this power and every living German would feel the consequences.

▶ *You are there* – Imagine yourself living in this earlier Germany. You are devoted to a church which has helped you to accept otherwise inexplicable events, like the sudden death of loved ones, and protected you from evils (like demons). You know that if you follow their teachings and act with charity you would eventually get into heaven. Now, imagine the impact when you discover that a respected professor of theology is teaching that the church has been wrong in its doctrines, corrupt for centuries and interested only in your money. Would you be amazed to discover that noblemen, princes and even other churchmen believe him? What would you think? In any case, you could not have ignored him.

Second, Luther's timing was inconvenient. Tetzel's indulgences were being used to raise money, but only indirectly for the stated reason of rebuilding St Peter's Cathedral in Rome. All money went first into the coffers of Albrecht of Brandenburg, archbishop of Mainz, so he could pay off his debts. Can you imagine his reaction when he got a copy of Luther's *Theses*?

Third, Luther appealed to German national pride. The *Theses* was immediately translated into German, printed and distributed far and wide. It proved that Germans were being tricked into handing over their life savings to a foreign power, at a time when Germans were becoming more self-aware as Germans. For these three reasons, Albrecht appealed to Leo X to silence Luther, and three attempts were made:

1. through the Augustinians
2. through debate with Cardinal Cajetan
3. through debate with Johann Eck.

Understanding why this failed
Simply put, the church authorities misunderstood the real threat and mistimed their response.

First, in April 1518, Luther was able to convince the Augustinians that he was right, thereby gaining a powerful and international monastic order to his side. Second, after refusing a papal summons to appear at Rome, he agreed to meet Tomas de Vio (Cardinal Cajetan), a papal representative, in October at Augsburg. Luther was willing to retract his arguments *if* he could be shown scriptural passages which proved him wrong. Cajetan argued that the pope need prove nothing. As God's agent, it was his inalienable right to interpret the Bible *as he saw fit*. This was a mistake.

▶ *You are there* – Imagine yourself as an educated and proud German. What would you make of this? Here was Luther arguing, in a logical and reasonable way, that the church was making a mistake and that you were being taken advantage of by foreign authorities. In reply, the pope's agent offered no justifications for it, other than claiming the church's rights and demanding your obedience. How would you feel about this?

Cajetan, inadvertently, turned Luther into a German folk hero. Yet, had the authorities done nothing further, things might have died down. Instead, a third attempt was made to silence Luther. This was another mistake.

The authorities challenged his arguments in open debate, which was what he originally wanted! They summoned him to Leipzig in July 1519 to face Johann Eck, a skilled academic. Eck forced Luther to examine his claims in finer detail, and intellectually humiliated him. It was too little too late, however. The issue was no longer an intellectual one, having worked its way into the German soul and, thus, beyond logic. Eck, inadvertently, turned a folk hero into a national saviour. Most importantly, however, he had forced Luther to take his theories to their logical conclusions.

Understanding why the logical element is important
Logic became the basis of Luther's entire theology. The logical extension of testing one aspect of papal power against scripture was

to test every aspect. The next step from this was to ask whether anything other than scripture (the very Word of God itself) was necessary. The church now made its final mistake. In June 1520, Luther was excommunicated.

▶ *You are there* – As a proud German, you now have a choice to make. Do you support the folk hero and national saviour who was only ever really doing his job, pointing out mistakes and asking that Germans be treated fairly. Or do you support the foreign papacy, which seemed interested only in money and unquestioning obedience?

Why Luther rejected other traditional religious ideas

There were three reasons for his doing so. He rejected them because they were:

1. not logically consistent with scripture
2. not logically consistent with God's power
3. not logically consistent with themselves.

What had prompted such considerations?
Early in his career (*c.*1510) Luther went to Rome. Witnessing the decadence of the papacy he began a serious inquiry into its claims of authority, especially on salvation, the sacraments and the intercessory role of the priesthood. Like everyone else, he feared the tortures of purgatory and, like everyone else, he had terrifying doubts about the possibility of salvation. In 1510, he believed (like everyone else) that the church and the pope could spare him pain and anguish but, unlike most others, Luther saw first-hand how corrupt and materialistic the church and its officials actually were and resolved to take action.

Luther developed a logical, scriptural alternative through which a thorough rejuvenation of Christian society could be achieved. This can be summed up in two phrases:

(a) *sola scriptura*, meaning that scripture was the only source of truth

(b) *solafideism* or *justification by faith alone*, meaning that salvation resulted merely by believing in God's promise of grace through the sacrifice of Jesus.

Why is this significant?
It was simple, logical, free and a great relief for those who feared purgatory and suffered doubts. Luther had a perfectly tenable theological presupposition (God's omnipotence) which made the conclusions practically self-evident. Thus:

1. Mankind can do absolutely nothing to secure its own salvation except have faith (thus, much existing traditions were, in fact, non-essential financial burdens).

2. Roman priests were irrelevant as, in God's eyes, all people were equal in the Church and faith – a *priesthood of all believers*.

This was an attractive alternative. It appealed to scholars, peasants and noblemen alike. Moreover, it appeared at a time when Germans wanted more control of their own church. Luther's ideas thus spread rapidly outward and, as a result, monasteries emptied, clergymen married and the Mass was abolished in several areas. The uniformity of Catholic worship was replaced by a bewildering variety of 'reformed' churches (which we will examine below).

Luther's understanding of the sacraments

Traditionally, there were seven sacraments, as seen in Chapter 2. Luther rejected confirmation, ordination, unction, matrimony and questioned penance, based on two reasons:

(a) Since logic dictated that everyone was equally a member of the community of the faithful, what need was there for priests imposing themselves between God and believers?

(b) Since all seven sacraments could not be proven exclusively by scripture, they could not all be divine.

Rome might have been prepared to overlook even this, except for the fact that the denial of ordination and penance had such serious consequences.

Ordination, obviously, was at the heart of the Roman hierarchy and, as only priests could make direct contact with God, they needed special legal status. Luther could find no scriptural justification for this, however. He concluded that all people have the same priestly powers, and only through the consent of the entire community could certain people exercise those powers for the sake of all. Just as neither priests nor popes have the power to forgive sin on God's behalf, so is penance similarly meaningless. Yes, confession and absolution have personal benefit, prayers and good works are good for the community, but only God can forgive sin. Luther also objected to the way penance had been used to ensure moral and law-abiding behaviour. By denying penance as a sacrament, Luther undermined priests as the dispensers of divine pardon and forgiveness, thus removing their special status.

▶ *You are there* – Imagine yourself as a member of a small, tight-knit early modern community, almost tribal in nature. A priest could withhold absolution, deny God's forgiveness and remove you from the fellowship of the church through excommunication. How would you function in society without personal interaction? No one would talk to you, no one would trade with you and you could not attend church services. What would you be willing to do to get back into the priest's (and hence God's) good graces? Could priests avoid abusing this power?

How else was Luther's denial of these five sacraments significant?
His denial had religious, social and political consequences. As it was clear to Luther that the papacy and the Roman church would not police itself and correct these abuses, he called upon temporal rulers to make the corrections. He thus overturned the usual church–state relationship and, through scriptural passages, completely undermined the Roman church's claims to power. The consequences were great:

Martin Luther

(a) As all believers are equal in the eyes of God, status must merely be a matter of office and function as bestowed (or removed!) by the community, so why not have temporal authorities correct spiritual abuses?

(b) Without consent, there is no basis for the claim that only the pope can interpret scripture, extrapolate divine law and summon general councils.

Luther's thinking on the eucharist and baptism

Although both the eucharist and baptism were clearly justified in scripture, Luther's interpretation was consistent with his own theology. Although he accepted the traditional Roman interpretation of baptism, he denied that a priest is specifically needed to perform it. Luther held that the person performing the act was merely a vessel of divine power and, therefore, any true believer could baptise. Baptism was an introduction to the community of the faithful and not a sacrament conferring grace upon the recipient. Luther's thinking on the eucharist is similar, but more complex.

Like the Romans, Luther believed in the *real presence* in the wine and bread. However, he denied that grace was conferred through participation in the ceremony, and denied that the priest performed any miracles. He also rejected the idea of withholding the wine from the laity, as this was merely another measure of separation between them and the clergy. By giving the sacrament *in both kinds* to all participants, the idea that all believers were of equal worth was reinforced. Moreover, he wanted the service conducted in the vernacular (native language) as this involved everybody. Luther published a German service in 1526.

If the priest performed no miracle, how were the bread and wine changed?
This is an important question but requires a subtle answer. **Transubstantiation** depends on the philosophical acceptance that there were two aspects to the reality of objects – mental and physical. The physical aspect or 'accident', is the substance immediately apparent to the senses, while the mental aspect or 'essence' is that more intangible quality that everyone seems to understand.

▶ *Picturing the scene* – Imagine an early modern table. The 'accident' of the table is wood. You know, of course, that not everything made of wood is a table. The 'essence' of the table (as everyone knows) clearly differentiates it from, say, a plank, a stool or a chair. While the accident of a table, a plank, a stool, a chair, a tree, are all wood, their essences allow you to differentiate (by sight, touch, etc.).

In the traditional view, therefore, during the Mass it was the essence of the bread and the wine which was transformed by the priest into the flesh and blood of Jesus, the accidents remaining unchanged and clearly visible as bread and wine. Luther rejected this in favour of (what *later* historians termed) **consubstantiation** (meaning 'co-existence'), the philosophical possibility that more than one element could be present in any object at any time. Thus, the bread remains bread (its essence has not changed) but the body of Jesus co-exists with it at the same time and in the same space. The priest did not perform a miracle of transformation; the *real presence* came to share the space in some other mysterious way, which Luther never explained.

▶ *Picturing the scene* – Imagine a blacksmith and an iron rod. The rod remains an iron rod even when it is heated in the fire, even when it is red hot. The rod and the fire share the space. The blacksmith does not put the fire into the rod, he is merely the instrument by which the rod is put into the fire.

The doctrine of *sola scriptura*

Luther held the Bible as the only religious authority, and had been willing to yield to Cajetan only if he could cite scriptural evidences as support. In his view, the church had been wrong to ascribe to the pope the inalienable right to confirm or determine the meaning of scripture, based on traditions, canons and the ancient Fathers. The Bible (scripture, the 'Word') became, for Luther, the test of what was legitimate.

Martin Luther

Who decides what a particular passage means?
This was a serious problem, as evinced by the many different interpretations already available to Germans. Luther thought scripture could interpret itself (if it were logically consistent with its own central message – the example of Jesus). If it were read sincerely, the Holy Spirit and right reason would make the sense of the scripture plain to the true believer. He was sure, however, that the Romans had misinterpreted it. It must be said, bluntly, that if scriptural passages could be interpreted in a way which confirmed Luther's theory of *justification by faith alone* then, he reasoned, it must be correct.

Could all passages be interpreted to Luther's liking?
Clearly not. For this reason he found certain books of the Bible less 'apostolic' or less 'canonical' than others. So, while St Paul's Epistle to the Romans (which could be interpreted to Luther's liking) was valuable, the Epistle of St James was not (as it could not be interpreted to fit Luther's theology). As Revelation did not deal with salvation anyway, Luther remained neutral. Although this is rather circular logic, he insisted that scripture must, no matter what else, be available for everyone to interpret and understand for themselves, so that they could live in a good Christian manner.

Two reasons for this are particularly important. The Roman interpretation was clearly error-ridden and they barely used the Bible in their services anyway. Yes, a few key passages were utilised (in Latin) but these were poorly understood and, thus, ill-used. For Luther, it was the role of the priest to help each person to make direct contact with God for themselves and to help everyone understand the Bible in a language they could all comprehend. Therefore, he set out to translate it into German and in conformity with his own understanding.

Understanding why Luther's translation is significant

Unlike previous translations, Luther used commonplace metaphors to make sure that ordinary Germans understood the message and could apply it to their own lives. He also used numerous wood cuts so that even the illiterate could be taught. He placed Bible stories into contemporary German settings, used contemporary language and phrasing, thereby standardising the German language and, hence, providing a real boon to German nationalism and society. He also recognised that people would need historical skills and linguistic guidelines to help their readings, so he set about to change German educational institutions, set up new ones and encouraged preaching. He even wrote guide books, for example a *Large Catechism* aimed at adults and a *Small Catechism* and primers aimed at children.

Was everything without a basis in scripture rendered illegitimate?
No. For Luther, if the Bible did not absolutely forbid something outright it should be discontinued only by common sense and community need. For instance, if everyone thought that paintings in the church distracted from listening to the sermon, the paintings could be removed (or priests could marry, or monasteries could be dissolved, etc.).

The meaning of the 'priesthood of all believers'

Luther wrote that all people are consecrated priests through baptism. He denied any special powers gained through ordination. Priests were not a caste apart; they carried no surplus of holiness or grace. They are merely those representatives of the community elected to do a particular job as teachers, preachers, guides and advisors on spiritual matters. He thought each community could choose a 'scholarly and devout citizen' to fulfil the role, and these would be aided by others and supported by the church.

Luther wanted an elected priesthood?
Initially yes, but he soon abandoned the idea as unworkable, and fell back on the familiar methods of patronage. He had already called on temporal authority figures to begin the reformation of abused practices, so appointing priests in their territorial churches was merely another task. As to who would be picked, Luther wrote about 'vocations' and 'callings' to the ministry in both inward (conscious) and outward ways, assuming such persons would make themselves known to the community and the authorities.

But, if everyone was equally a priest, why retain the office at all?
It was merely a matter of function, even the word 'priesthood' itself (with its Roman implications) was dropped in favour of the word 'ministry', which much better described a group of specialist functionaries anyway. Thus, whereas a priest led, ordered or shepherded a community, a minister offered comfort and served the community. They also preached, helped others to interpret scripture, dispensed the sacraments in a proper fashion and performed other common pastoral functions. Moreover, ministers had to be much better qualified as both educators and pastors. Their authority would be recognised and granted through the community's guardians, its temporal rulers, as now the church was nothing more than the gathering of the faithful in any one place, be it a kingdom or an independent city-state.

Understanding the wider political implications
Obviously, the civil authorities themselves would be very favourable to the idea of their own expanded spiritual authority. Without the church establishing a separate and inviolate rule of its own, the civil power would be all the greater.

▶ *You are there* – Imagine yourself as an early modern civil authority figure. While you would certainly encourage Luther's reforms, would you support them because they were right or because they tended to increase your personal power and wealth?

For Luther, the 'whys' were unimportant, provided that the old, false, Roman hierarchy was eliminated and good order maintained. Unfaithful rulers would face God's judgement in the end.

Why Luther rejected traditional salvation doctrine

To understand his thinking, we have to break it down into the five traditional aspects of salvation theology and deal with these separately.

With regard to sin, Luther went further than traditional 'original sin' thinking, which held that humans became predisposed toward sin of all kinds. He thought that, indeed, humans could no longer even distinguish good from evil. Man has no free will, no moral free choice and is thus free only *to* sin. Man must also recognise his sinful nature, but Luther rejected as absurd the traditional belief that upholding divine laws mitigated the guilt. Only faith in divine grace would bring salvation. Luther held faith (the second aspect) to be a composite of knowledge, assent and trust. Traditionally, faith was passive. It consisted of listening to a sermon, obeying the priests and relying on them to act as go-betweens with God. Luther insisted on active faith: the true believer must truly understand what was happening and participate in a positive way. The believer must truly learn and have a perfect knowledge of his sinful nature and of God's saving grace.

Another aspect was regeneration which, for Luther, was more than a mere recognition of sinfulness. The true believer must also change his life to reflect his awareness, live as a true Christian, unconcerned with good works, rewards and punishments. Two attributes are central. One is repentance, not the traditional Roman sacrament of penance and all it stood for, but a complete change of heart. Repentance should be the sign that the penitent is living a new life in the traditional virtues for the good of the entire community of believers, regardless of social position, occupation or wealth. The second is the removal of the fear of death and purgatory, since the repentant go to heaven, where all mysteries were solved.

With regard to the fourth aspect, predestination, Luther stressed a dual distinction. 'God revealed' called to all believers to repent and have faith, and offered free grace to all. 'God hidden', however, chose the saved and the damned at creation. That this was so could be plainly observed as some people seemed naturally charitable while others seemed naturally villainous. Salvation could not be earned by man, only granted by God. Why some are saved and some damned is a mystery which, of course, no mortal could understand (true faith). While this certainly seems unfair, Luther also stressed that God was not the cause of evil either.

Understanding the impact of Luther's salvation theory
In a phrase, the impact of Luther's salvation theory was 'social upheaval'.

▶ *You are there* – Try to imagine how your own life would have changed. Pre-Luther, you confessed, did penance, heard Mass and received the sacraments without question because the priests told you to. You did good works and confessed because some of your guilt would be washed away. You bought indulgences and gave money to the Church, an organisation well beyond your comprehension, because you needed the intervention of the priests with God. You feared death because you feared the penalties of purgatory and the punishments of hell, but you could never be sure of salvation either. Post-Luther, you learned for yourself what it meant to be a Christian. You no longer feared death or agonised over mysteries. You were secure in the knowledge that grace was the free gift of God. You needed only to believe. Which sounds better?

Luther's doctrine of 'justification by faith alone'

This fifth aspect of salvation will be considered apart from the others as it is the single most important aspect of Luther's theology of salvation. Moreover, justification is the core principle of Christian doctrine and the one which really sets the reformers apart. To Luther, *justification by faith alone* meant two things.

1. It meant that the guilt of sin was unconditionally washed away by God's free grant of grace.

2. It meant that the Holy Spirit regenerated the sinner's soul, by which the sinner could begin to act in a morally virtuous manner (was 'born again').

Justification by faith alone therefore meant exactly that – no need for priests as go-betweens, no need for good works or acts of charity – the Christian is saved by faith and nothing else.

The impact of Luther

Inadvertent or not, Luther transformed early modern Germany in spiritual, social and political ways. As the emperor was little more than a figurehead, people looked to their regional rulers for change, leadership and solutions to social, economic and religious problems. As a result, state churches emerged. Each had a prince or urban magistracy at its head, and the temporal rulers gained a substantial degree of near-autonomous authority. Between 1525 and 1526, the elector of Saxony organised a state 'Lutheran' Church. His example was repeated by other rulers in Ansbach, Hesse and ducal Prussia soon after.

Luther's impact was also negative, however. 'Utopian' social revolutionaries had taken his message and interpreted it as a general attack on the privileged classes, like the clergy or nobility. Moreover, Luther had helped place the Bible into the hands of the semi-educated, and this spawned ever more radical interpretations and movements, as we shall see. These negative influences culminated in the great 'peasant revolt' in southern and central Germany of 1525–6, which resulted in little more than 75,000 peasant deaths and social chaos. Over the next three decades, solutions were attempted, including:

(a) the *Augsburg Confession* (1530), which was an attempt to find a compromise and truce between Lutherans and Roman Catholics

(b) the establishment of the League of Schmalkalden (1531) to defend Protestantism

(c) the *Augsburg Settlement* (1555), which ended religious war and enshrined two principles – future religious disputes would be settled by law and *cuius regio, eius religio* ('who rules, his religion').

Did all Germans benefit from the Settlement?
The peasants gained nothing, but the creation of established Lutheran churches with a married, well-educated clergy,

represented substantial growth for the middle classes. The clergy, with its interests in status and property, and therefore stability, reinforced the middling rank. The nobles gained power, but became less dogmatic and more attached to the ways of compromise in religion and politics.

Tutorial

Summary of key ideas

Justification by faith alone – Logic and scripture indicated for Luther that man can have no role in, or impact upon, his own salvation. He can only have faith. It depends solely on the will of God as a free gift granted to all believers without the mediation of priests. For Luther, faith included an element of trust in the promise of God, made through the sacrifice of Jesus (which produced a reservoir of grace enabling God arbitrarily to ignore the sinfulness of those who believed).

Priesthood of all believers – Luther held that both logic and scripture dictate that all believers are equal in the eyes of God. All are of the same religious status and merely distinguished by function. As people need no mediator between themselves and God, they are their own priests.

Sola scriptura – For Luther, scripture, as the Word of God, was the sole validation of religious doctrine. No institution was needed for interpretative guidance. Anyone inspired by the Holy Spirit would discover the meaning of the passages for themselves.

Baptism – A true sacrament which provided no grace, but reminded the recipient of God's saving power.

The eucharist – This was a true sacrament which provided no grace, no miracles, but which contained the *real presence* of Jesus. The bread and wine were not transformed into the body and blood but co-existed through the power of God's promise alone.

Progress questions
1. How did the church authorities' response to Luther give credence to his complaints?

2. What is the difference between Luther's doctrine of the eucharist and the traditional Catholic doctrine?

3. Why did Luther place such critical importance on the Bible?

Seminar discussion
1. Did Luther really work out his theological positions in a logical manner, each following and complementing the last?

2. How were Luther's doctrines dangerous for the Roman Catholic Church?

Practical assignments
1. Make a chart of several columns, listing Lutheran doctrines in the first and lists of how these impacted upon early modern German religion, society, politics, economics, nationalism or anything else you can imagine in the others.

2. Imagine yourself living at the time as a Catholic priest. Write a letter to the pope listing how Luther's doctrines are dangerous. Write a reply offering advice on how to oppose them.

Study and revision tips
1. If you are making notes on the indulgences crisis and Luther's *Ninety-Five Theses*, for instance, consider a chronological chart of three columns – date, event, response.

2. Create a simple chronological chart to help you visualise the events. Include the high points of Luther's career such as personal events, writings, debates and events out of his control (like the Peasants' War).

3. Using two columns, make a list of the five sacraments Luther denied in one and list his reasons for denying them in the other.

4

The Urban Reformers

One minute summary – A G Dickens said that the reformation was an 'urban event'. He meant that, without the towns and cities and what they represent – collections of humanity, higher literacy, political awareness and social sophistication – the reformation might have had little real impact. In many ways, the reformation had only succeeded because of favourable collective decisions by populations convinced of the righteousness and opinions of one or more preachers among them. Collectively, they pressured local leaders (sometimes the only political authorities) for change, or the leaders initiated programmes for their own reasons. Clearly, we cannot look at all the possibilities, so three of the better cases have been selected. This chapter will help you to understand:

▶ the socio-political context of urban reformation movements
▶ Zwingli's impact on Zürich
▶ Bucer's impact on Strasbourg
▶ Oecolampadius's impact on Basel
▶ how their theologies contrasted with each other's and with Luther's
▶ the urban reform programmes of Bucer, Oecolampadius and Zwingli.

The social and political context

When historians say that the reformation was largely urban-based, they mean that fifty or so imperial cities responded positively to religious change, and that it spread across the Swiss Confederacy through a process of public debate and treaty obligations. There were also several isolated incidents in the urban centres of France, Spain, Italy and elsewhere. Success or failure depended on a number of urban political and social factors.

Understanding these factors

By the early sixteenth century, the city councils of the imperial cities had managed to gain nominal independence. Councils functioned as governments and dealt with their subjects' grievances and other more serious problems. These included:

- a too rapid population expansion
- extended food crises linked with the ravages of the Black Death
- several agrarian crises
- rural depopulation – agricultural workers migrated to the cities
- urban discontent – for example, trade guilds restricting new memberships.

Our period witnessed growing social unrest in many cities. Demands for broader-based and more representative governments were gaining momentum. In many cases, the ideas of the reformers became linked with these demands for change. Examining the results and responses helps us to understand why reform succeeded in some places but failed in others.

Success or failure depended upon community responses to problems. Cities where the reformation failed faced the growing social tensions and restored order through a renewed reliance upon external political bodies, like the imperial government or the papal curia.

Where the reformation succeeded, tensions had sometimes been resolved by adopting Luther's doctrine of the 'priesthood of all believers'. This broke down traditional barriers. It encouraged a sense of communal unity and bound inhabitants together in a shared religious life. Moreover, accepting the doctrine of 'justification by faith alone' eased tensions inherent in the late medieval penitential system. Strasbourg gives us a different scenario in that the reformation was used to resolve the tensions of severe class struggle. The ruling coalition of patricians and merchants held that their social positions could be maintained only through alignment with the reformers, so brought in reform as a subtle means of preserving vested interests.

The Urban Reformers

▶ *You are there* – Your life as an early modern urbanite is stressful indeed. So many people, so many problems! Try to imagine the sheer mental relief offered by the message of the reformers. 'Justification by faith alone' eliminated the financial burden of indulgences, good works and charity, and the psychological pressure of purgatory. Would you go along with this, or turn to imperial troops?

Success of the reformation in the cities was, obviously, never certain. It came to depend upon certain pre-conditions:

(a) some form of popular pressure for change (social, religious, etc)

(b) historical contingencies (like existing treaties) with other cities

(c) the city councils' willingness to accept change for whatever reason.

In practice, therefore, the relationship between council and reformer was largely symbiotic. The reformer presented a coherent vision of the Christian gospel; the council saw the religious, social and political implications. By the 'reformer' we mean here Bucer, Zwingli or Oecolampadius. They gave religious direction to a movement which, unchecked and lacking in direction, might have degenerated into chaos. It might have fallen under the authority of political masters jealous of their own powers and often hoping to extend reform beyond the programme of the reformer.

Therefore, the relation between reformer and council was delicate. It was easily prone to disruption, with real power permanently in the hands of the council.

The reformers and their cities

Soon after Erasmus published his *Greek New Testament*, its importance was realised by other humanists. Although these men were diverse in character, most of them came from the independent urban areas. Most were well-educated theologians and ordained clergymen. They began to examine the issues for themselves, or soon did so after admitting the logic of Luther's own theories.

▶ Ulrich Zwingli (1484–1531) was influenced by Erasmus. As a native of Switzerland he shared the long-standing native antipathy toward all things German. He constantly denied any influence by Luther. Zwingli was a parish priest in the small town of Glarus (*c*.1506–16), where he combined routine work with intensive studies of Latin, Greek and Hebrew. In time (*c*.1518) he moved to Zürich and pursued his own ideas. He tested every new theory against Jesus, arriving at almost exactly the Lutheran position on most issues.

▶ Johannes Hussgen, or Oecolampadius (1482–1531), was a Swabian, and had been employed by Erasmus on the Bible translation. He was later influenced by Luther to leave his monastery (*c*.1522) and pursue religious reform as a preacher in Basel. He bridged the gap between Luther and Zwingli, following one or the other on specific issues.

▶ Martin Bucer (1491–1551) of Alsace was a Dominican studying theology at Heidelberg. As part of the humanist circle there he was influenced by Erasmus but, having witnessed the Luther episode at the Augustinian chapter (1518), left his monastery, married a runaway nun (1522) and moved to Strasbourg.

The selection of these three also allows us to compare and contrast the reformation in three different geographic locations:

> Zürich – a typical town of the Swiss Confederation
> Strasbourg – an independent imperial German city
> Basel – a city on the Swiss-German border.

Example 1 – Zwingli's impact on Zürich

Zwingli's impact was initially uncertain because of the power of the city fathers and his own political naiveté. Although nominally under the authority of the bishop of Constance, the city fathers actually controlled religion because the bishop's authority was weak and opposed by most of the local clergy.

Once Zwingli acknowledged the need to convince the council of the necessity of each change, reform progressed. By 1525, a new baptismal order had been devised. Objections had been raised against images and crucifixes in the churches (images were removed), and against the Mass (a new order was prepared by Zwingli). Some monasteries were dissolved.

Example 2 – Bucer's impact on Strasbourg
Bucer's impact on Strasbourg was, individually, marginal but, as a part of the humanist reform movement, it was great. This is largely because the city was open to all ideas and peoples as a means of self-protection from imperial intervention. As in Zürich, the ruling council was a mixture of patricians and guildmen.

Bucer published a formal statement of reform in 1524, the same year the first vernacular Mass and baptism was celebrated, although Mass would be forbidden thereafter. Communion in both kinds was offered to the laity. Monasteries were closed down in 1529. In 1536, influenced by Bucer's further writings, the city subscribed formally to Lutheran theology.

Example 3 – Oecolampadius' impact on Basel
In brief, Oecolampadius influenced Basel into Zwinglian-type reform. The year 1525 witnessed the secularisation of the monasteries, Roman church festivals were abolished in 1527 and the Mass abolished in 1529.

Theological contrasts

We have already examined Luther's theology of the sacraments and salvation, as well as his thoughts on the scripture and church–state relations, and will not be repeating them. Luther does, however, form the basis of our comparison (review Chapter 3).

The urban reformers' theologies of salvation
Influenced by humanist practices and Erasmus's translation, the urban reformers, like Luther, became convinced that many church teachings were either positively incorrect or clearly lacking in Biblical justification. Like Luther, they came to believe that ordinary people were being misled and were heading for damna-

tion. As regards salvation, all the reformers ascribed the *faith alone* view, but with slight disagreements in the details.

Where Luther, for instance, discussed the guilt of original sin, Zwingli and Bucer spoke instead of the 'disease'. They wanted to integrate the claim that man had no choice in the matter, but without casting blame on God. On faith, we know that Luther spoke of a composite of knowledge, assent and trust, whereby the believer learned and gained a perfect knowledge of his sinful nature and of God's saving grace. We saw him use 'sin' and 'law' as God's means of humbling humans into recognising their low state. Zwingli challenged this view that the 'law' caused misery, pointing to human weakness in the face of the law instead. It is a subtle difference.

▶ *Picturing the scene* – Zwingli described the law as a light shining upon a sinner, a deformed man. Luther held that the light intensified the deformity, while Zwingli held that the light merely illuminated it.

Moreover, Luther wanted Christians to listen, be taught and to learn for themselves in a positive manner. Zwingli resolved, instead, to teach people how to secure salvation for themselves.

As the Bible contained a complete statement of God's intentions for humanity, all people really needed was a proper explanation. What was not supported by the Bible was declared invalid. The central issue of faith was, of course, understanding Jesus's sacrifice. Zwingli called this a 'pledge' or 'seal' of grace to general agreement. The problem became Jesus himself. Traditional dogma held that he was 'truly God and truly man' (two natures combined but not commingled). Luther, Oecolampadius and Bucer explained this in largely traditional ways, it not being a great concern for them. It was, however, an issue for Zwingli, who wanted the distinction between the two natures more clearly defined. For him, it must be clearer that it was the 'human' nature of Jesus which suffered, not the 'divine' nature.

We noted that justification theology was a key issue and Luther's theory was widely supported. The main difference is that while Luther focused on the 'individual', Zwingli was more interested in

The Urban Reformers

the 'community' (of Zürich) as a whole and more interested in moral renewal and regeneration of the institutions, rather than merely forgiveness of individual sinners. Moreover, Luther seems to say that the believer need perform no moral actions; Zwingli found this absurd.

▶ *Picturing the scene* – Imagine yourself seeking salvation. Luther explains God's promises to the believer in an attempt to console and reassure; 'God sent Jesus for your sins..', you need do nothing but believe. Zwingli explains, after the example of Jesus, what moral actions God demands of the believer.

It is vague, despite his claims, just how independent from Luther Zwingli actually was. Bucer attempted a compromise with a doctrine called 'double justification'. He wrote that there were two stages – justification of the ungodly (God's free forgiveness of human sin) and justification of the godly (the obedient human response to moral commandments). Jesus provided the external model which, with help from the Holy Spirit, believers were to emulate. Clearly, Bucer's 'justification of the godly' would seem to echo Luther's understanding of regeneration of the true believer as a 'change of life' to reflect his new self-awareness. While their descriptions may differ somewhat, Bucer, Zwingli and Oecolampadius were basically of the same position.

On predestination, however, there was little real difference all around. Luther's distinction between 'God revealed' and 'God hidden' was generally upheld, save that Zwingli emphasised God's 'mercy' and 'justice' in election. In order to avoid blaming God for the evil of damned sinners, Bucer held with Luther's silence on the mystery, while both Oecolampadius and Zwingli taught that only the elect (a majority of humans) were truly predestined; the damned (a tiny minority) were merely allowed to sin. Like Luther, Oecolampadius thought it best to avoid the subject when preaching. Bucer thought that preaching it would strengthen faith, while Zwingli speculated much but offered few solid answers.

The urban reformers' use of scripture

Luther's theory of *sola scriptura* was a sensible approach; scripture contains everything people need for salvation, let common sense and logic take care of the rest. Generally, the urban reformers shared this view. Again, where differences appear they are slight and more to do with the reformers' personal experiences. Zwingli, for example, disliked the idea of 'prioritising' books according to 'apostolicity'. He was, therefore, less willing to allow that anything not in the Bible was a matter for common sense. Moreover, whereas Luther looked for the literal sense (what is written), the 'humanist' urban reformers recognised other possibilities requiring interpretation of what was actually written, including:

- allegory – symbolic meanings
- tropology – moral/ethical or figurative meanings
- anagogy – prophetic meanings.

We shall see that this recognition has particular relevance as regards the sacraments.

The urban reformers' doctrines of the sacraments

Here, Luther and the urban reformers share a great deal, such as definitions and expectations. For example, they all held that sacraments were little more than public declarations of intent to join the community of the faithful. Zwingli was particularly zealous here and it led him into difficulties with more radical theologians over infant baptism. How could he argue against adult baptism when, clearly, only adults have a publicly demonstrable faith?

As Zwingli regarded original sin as a disease rather than as guilt to be washed away, infants had no inherent sinfulness, so he could not hide behind the Roman tradition that baptism purged guilt. He solved this dilemma by concentrating on the community. Infant baptism became a token of membership in the community and a demonstration of loyalty to it (the criterion of the loyal citizen). We shall see how the Anabaptists used Zwingli's thinking on this point for their own ends (Chapter 5). The greater issue of contention was the eucharist, particularly over the 'real presence'.

Zwingli (and Oecolampadius) and Luther seriously dissented on one rather minor point in their eucharistic doctrines, but this was enough to drive a stake of irreconcilable hatred between them, despite Bucer's attempted mediations. The point? One phrase in the Bible. Where Jesus is reported as saying (as he broke the bread at the Last Supper) 'Eat, this *is* my body', Luther (as noted earlier) took this literally, while denying **transubstantiation**. Zwingli rejected the argument altogether that Jesus had meant the words literally. Instead, he argued that the words had been used only figuratively. The word 'is', for Zwingli, meant 'represents'.

For him, the recipients of the bread and wine are simply remembering Jesus's sacrifice and celebrating their own resulting salvation. As such, the ceremony had little real significance otherwise. What the student needs to appreciate, however, was just how radical this shift in thinking was. For Zwingli, the power of collective worship was not in bringing Jesus's physical being down to the congregation (the material objects hold no holy power). Rather it lay in raising their own spirits up into contact with Jesus in heaven. What Zwingli was truly interested in was preparing people for that spiritual connection.

▶ *You are there* – Imagine yourself attending the eucharist in Zwingli's Zürich. Forget the philosophical niceties; the bread is merely bread and the wine is merely wine. By participating, you are reminding yourself that Jesus's sacrifice was for your benefit and that you are saved. You are not drawing God down to you, God is already there all around you.

Bucer, with some other humanists, tried to adopt a middling position between these two 'extremes'. He viewed the eucharist as a commemorative act in which the recipients entered into a real communion with Jesus.

The urban reform programmes

Bucer, Oecolampadius and Zwingli

All our sample reformers understood the church as a 'community of the faithful' or 'of true believers'. Moreover, as no one knew precisely who was 'elect' and who was 'damned', all spoke of the church 'visible' and 'invisible'. The former was the gathering of all professed believers, while the latter was only the elect. Whatever small disagreements they had on these issues, they agreed that human institutions (and humans) cannot be allowed as the 'head' of the church or as the hierarchy of its leadership. They generally agreed on a *priesthood of all believers* type equality, on the need for ministers rather than priests, the rejection of apostolic succession, on the role of the ministers and on the need for civilian education. Where they differed was in trying to bring temporal authorities into the equation.

They all held that the community was the aggregate of all local churches. What was local was defined by the closest political unit, for example a city, a noble estate, or kingdom. But how were the political and spiritual authorities related?

Luther, the product of a small Saxon town under the thumb of the local prince, was quite happy to give the duke (as the temporal authority) power over the church (Chapter 3). He viewed the two authorities as separate, but connected through their common memberships. Since his concern was the individual rather than the community as a whole and, since magistrates and ministers only differed by community perception, Luther could see no problem in subordinating ecclesiastical matters to temporal figures – a logical, sensible and realistic view.

Zwingli, Bucer and Oecolampadius were all products of free-cities where councils supervised church matters, so held the temporal and ecclesiastical as undifferentiated, both serving God's rule over the community. In other words, the two spheres were mixed but, for them, the temporal authorities had only the power to help the spiritual, not to direct it.

Because Zürich (for instance) was democratically controlled, Zwingli's reforms all had to have majority support in the council. He understood this, but failed to recognise the fact that the council saw itself as a political assembly rather than as the 'Christian' assembly he took it to be. For him, magistrates (the council) helped the ministers (or prophets) by passing secular laws consistent with the Bible, in order to ensure that the church was served by effective preachers. Conversely, the ministers helped the magistrates by

The Urban Reformers

handling the actual subject matter (preaching, doctrine) themselves. To Zwingli, it was clear that the council could not judge the Word of God as this was the role of the minister. If they did, he believed he was free to preach against them, even on economic or political matters.

In this, Zwingli was naive and he soon paid the price. In Zürich, the council was the final arbiter in all religious matters, and ministers were expected to obey. Likewise, Oecolampadius wanted the structures of church and state clearly separated. The spiritual members would police themselves through appropriately spiritual sanctions, while lay authority figures might be drafted in only to aid the church in certain disciplinary cases. Bucer wanted unique disciplinary powers guaranteed to the church without temporal interference. This too failed.

▶ *You are there* – Imagine yourself as a councillor in Zwingli's Zürich or Bucer's Strasbourg. You are told that your criteria for all policies must be submission to the Word of God, the assent of the church, peace and furtherance of the Gospel, but that you have no actual power of enforcement or determination of what this means in reality. As a politician, would you accept such limitations?

Tutorial

Summary of key ideas

Double justification – Bucer's understanding of salvation in two stages: (1) 'justification of the ungodly', which is God's offer of grace to all humans and forgiveness of all sin, and (2) 'justification of the godly', which is the obedient human response to God's moral commandments, similar to Luther's regeneration theory. For Bucer, Jesus becomes an external model for believers to emulate.

Infant baptism – Zwingli's defence against adult baptism. The sacrament is a symbol of loyalty to the community of God and a sign of application to it.

(The) eucharist – For Zwingli, it was a ceremony of remembrance wherein the *real presence* of Jesus is nominal as God is everywhere anyway.

Progress questions
1. Explain the difference between the urban reformers' theology of the sacraments and that of Luther.

2. Summarise and compare Zwinglian and Lutheran theology.

Seminar discussion
1. Were the urban reformers influenced more by Erasmus or Luther?

2. Why is the reformation's urban context seen as so important by historians?

Practical assignment
You will almost certainly never be asked a question dealing with any one of the urban reformers alone. Instead, you will encounter compare/contrast type questions (with Luther). To prepare, make a chart of several columns in which you can compare the beliefs, doctrines and influence(s) of the reformers and Luther (or Calvin).

Study and revision tips
1. Make a list of important reformation doctrines. List where the urban 'humanist' reformers differ from Luther.

2. Create a simple chart to help you visualise the specific reformation events in Basel, Zürich and Strasbourg.

5

Radical Reformation

One minute summary – Luther and the urban reformers represent rather moderate, slow, piecemeal movements but, as so often happens, where change is in the air some people want it immediately. Such were the Anabaptists. The name was a derogatory term of Zwingli's meaning 're-baptisers'. They held that only those who had made a personal public profession of faith should be baptised. It was the principle of *sola scriptura*, however, which distinguishes them. Where Luther or Zwingli accepted the necessity of non-scriptural practices, the radicals took the doctrine to mean the belief in, and practise of, *only* those things *explicitly* taught in scripture (all else being false). This chapter will help you to understand:

- why the Anabaptists are important but obscure
- why their key ideas were considered dangerous
- the meaning of *sola experientia* and spiritualism
- the importance of Thomas Müntzer
- the importance of the Münster affair.

Why the Anabaptists are important but obscure

The student of history is well aware of today's religious groups which eschew violence and abstain from modern technologies. We have all seen movies or television programmes featuring the Amish, Quakers or the Mennonites. Yet the origins of these pacifist and simple-living groups are among the most violent in history. This is why examining the Anabaptists is important. They are obscure for a number of reasons:

1. they were considered a left-wing lunatic fringe

2. they had no clear confessional statements
3. they had little real immediate impact
4. they founded no institutions
5. they left no readily assessable body of records
6. they produced relatively few significant theologians.

For these reasons, the radical groups get lumped together under the one label, however inappropriate this might be. Whatever opinions of them might now be – and this seems to depend on a variety of issues – all agree that to the early modern mind, they were the greatest threat to Christian society.

Why the Anabaptists were considered so dangerous

The simple answer is that their beliefs weakened the very basis of society – civil obedience – and undermined the traditional institutions of law and order. For example, in 1527 the governments of Zürich, Berne and St Gallen accused the Anabaptists of holding three anti-social beliefs:

1. that no true Christian can either give or receive interest or income on a sum of capital

2. that all temporal goods are free and common

3. that all people can have full property rights to all property.

For these and other reasons, the Anabaptists were considered very dangerous, by the wealthy middle classes in particular, and suffered violent suppression.

> ▶ *You are there* – Try to imagine your life in early modern Berne. You are law abiding, you pay your taxes and you expect your private property to be respected. How would you react to a group of people showing up one day, using your property and material possessions and claiming a divine right to do so? Would their 'holier-than-thou' attitude, on top of everything else, upset you further? What would you have your rulers do?

Radical Reformation

The radicals' key ideas

The religious groups that historians term 'radicals' were both ideologically and geographically diverse, but a number of common elements can be discerned with hindsight:

- a general distrust of external authorities
- the rejection of infant baptism in favour of the baptism of adult believers
- common ownership of property
- an emphasis upon pacifism and non-resistance (but a readiness to defend).

Behind it all is an unconventional vision of Christianity. Luther, Zwingli, Calvin and the Roman Catholics all agreed on certain basic premises (Chapter 2). These included a visible church, inclusive of all professed believers, coexistent with the local political community, and a mutually beneficial church–state relationship. The radicals, however, considered themselves, in their local congregations, completely apart from the state. Moreover, the one true church consisted only of true believers who had been tested and acknowledged as such (everyone else was banned).

Because of this, the wealthy, the rulers, the middle classes and the spiritual authorities all considered them a threat:

(a) they were disruptive of local social, political and religious codes
(b) they used the Bible in too literal a way (to logical extremes)
(c) they formed states within states, becoming civic liabilities wherever they went.

It was the second reason, their understanding of *sola scriptura*, which is important for our purposes.

Understanding the radical doctrine of baptism

As a student, make yourself familiar with the traditional interpretation of this sacrament. Understand its relation to original sin and how it was differently understood by Luther and Zwingli (review Chapters 2 to 4) in symbolic terms, as an analogy of the sacrifice of Jesus, a signal of the desire of individuals to join the church 'visible' or (for Zwingli) for parents to signal this on behalf of their children. This was to understand certain principles as defining of Christianity:

- one universal church with one unifying creed (theology)
- its visible and invisible aspects
- the mutually beneficial church–state relationship.

The radicals, however, understood Christianity differently. They defined it as:

- an exclusive community of voluntary members
- based on *sola scriptura* without compromise or prevarication
- with no state involvement, no mutual relationship (separation from civil power).

Thus, their understanding of baptism was also different.

For the moderates, baptism was an outward sign by which recipients were accepted into the community of the faithful. The radicals thought this absurd and a corruption of the true church. They understood baptism in a unique, three-fold manner:

(a) inner baptism – whereby the true believer recognises himself as the recipient of grace through the Holy Spirit leading him to repentance

(b) water baptism – administered to the truly faithful as a sign of their faith and renewed life as disciples of Jesus

(c) blood baptism or martyrdom – expected because true disciples are not of the material world and will face hatred and persecution.

Luther saw this as salvation turned upside down and smacking not a little of Pelagianism. As we saw, baptism was valid for Luther because it is based on a condition external to the believer – God's free grace. God chooses the truly faithful. For the radicals, baptism is

Radical Reformation

only valid if based on an internal condition – the truly faithful choose themselves. Since infants cannot recognise, much less articulate, internal spiritual renewal, only adult baptism is valid. Taken to its logical conclusion, radicals recognised that only the internal and spiritual mattered at all. The external and material, like the use of sacraments, could be discarded.

The radical doctrine of *sola experientia* or spiritualism

You may recognise both Luther and Zwingli as 'evangelicals', those who hold the Bible pre-eminent over human tradition. Moreover, they had been scholars struggling to find true meanings and squabbling over rival interpretations. All the reformers (so far) also relied on logic at the expense of emotion. The Anabaptists, few of whom were actually scholars, came to regard the Bible as secondary to God's direct communication with the individual believer through the Holy Spirit. They became mystics, prepared to recognise the validity of visions and inner voices. For them, the *experience* of faith was all important. Of course, by acknowledging visions and inner voices as the real 'Word' of God (even when in direct conflict with scripture) they left themselves exposed to skilful demagogues.

With this in mind, it is easy to see how the Anabaptist movement could splinter into even more radical sects. Some might teach that only belief itself was important (individual behaviour did not matter). Others might follow the long-established tradition of millenarianism, the belief that the end of the world and the second coming of Jesus was nigh. This led them to think they had nothing to do but wait patiently for it. Others still might be persuaded that the second coming would only take place once all non-believers were dead. These few, therefore, set about what they understood to be God's work with swords in hand and clear minds.

▶ *Picturing the scene* – You can easily understand the Anabaptist value system by bringing to mind any number of modern-day cults. Only those who share the beliefs of the local group are among the saved; outsiders need not be tolerated; members are segregated from the rest of the community into self-contained units; simplified forms of dress are worn; purified forms of speech are used; self-defence is made ready.

The Branch Dividians of Waco Texas are a good example of these features.

Such an attitude is sometimes labelled 'subversive piety' by historians. Most Anabaptists refused to recognise any authority other than God. They were therefore unwilling to do anything to support the usurpation of divine power by civil authorities. Accordingly they would not pay taxes, serve in the army, hold public office, or swear oaths of allegiance. Unsurprisingly, the authorities reacted negatively. They feared that the Anabaptists would encourage civil disobedience and the breakdown of traditional society. In other words, they encouraged revolt by their very existence and, consequently, extreme measures were taken against them. Two examples will serve as illustration:

(a) the example of Thomas Müntzer
(b) the Münster affair.

The importance of Thomas Müntzer

In a phrase, the importance of Thomas Müntzer was bad public relations. Müntzer (*c*.1489–1525), was one of the most notorious of the early radical-revolutionaries. His life highlights the political and religious consequences of spiritualism and experiential religion.

Müntzer was a well-educated parish priest and one of Luther's early supporters in Saxony, but became disillusioned with Luther's caution and disinterest in political and social issues. Around 1520 he moved to Zwickau and became involved in local class tensions, claiming to be led by the will of God. He soon broke with Luther and his theory of *justification by faith alone*, turning instead to mysticism and three-fold baptism. He preached that the second coming should be hastened by destroying the wicked (meaning the rich). He argued that their possessions should be confiscated and redistributed among the poor. Obviously, the council could not countenance such opinion and he was forced to leave. Müntzer wandered, developed his radical doctrines and eventually took up a preaching post in electoral Saxony (at Allstedt), much to general disapproval.

Frederick the Wise, however, was reluctant to punish a preacher until a clear case was proved against him. This tolerance allowed Müntzer to preach his beliefs for three more years, unhindered, spreading alarm among the rich and attracting great adverse publicity for the reforming cause. Hostile reports mounted and, finally, Frederick sent his brother to investigate. Exiled but undaunted, Müntzer carried on. The coming of the peasants' war allowed him to practise what he had preached, seeing it as the means whereby the godly could eliminate the godless, and so hasten the second coming. He became one of the leading exponents of mindless violence and destruction but, after leading his supporters to military defeat, he was captured, brutally tortured, and killed in 1525.

The importance of the city of Münster

This was even more bizarre and damaging to the Anabaptists' reputation than Müntzer's preaching. As a result of the social unrest caused by the peasants' war, the north-western German city of Münster became the target of the visionary Melchior Hoffman and a group of extremists of the Müntzer-type, known as Melchiorites.

Hoffman proclaimed himself the new Elijah (a Biblical prophet) and went first to Strasbourg, his 'new Jerusalem'. Although imprisoned for the rest of his life, he managed to sneak out some writings which filtered their way back to his supporters in Münster. They took up his message that the second coming and end of the world would happen in 1533. But, he cautioned, the ungodly must be destroyed *first* and that, as a result, the saints would rule the earth prior to the second coming, through co-operation between the 'prophet' and the 'pious ruler'.

By 1532, Münster was the focus of the social revolutionary activities of Bernard Rothmann, a priest, against its prince-bishop. Thousands of Anabaptist refugees flooded into the new 'evangelical city', escaping Dutch persecution, and managed to convert some of the city's leaders to the cause. This meant they could offer a rare safe haven to social revolutionaries of all kinds and especially to those who believed that blood must flow before Jesus would return. Citizens who did not share their views (the godless) either fled or were killed outright. Infant baptism was done away with and the Lord's Supper was celebrated with unconsecrated bread. The reaction of neighbouring princes, clerical and secular, Catholic and Protestant, was uniformly hostile. A combined army was raised and Münster was put under siege. What followed was truly bizarre.

The mantle of leadership was assumed by Jan Bockelson (Jan of Leiden), a Dutch tailor who claimed to be the 'voice of God'. Under his leadership, the Anabaptists managed to repel a major strike force. This allowed Jan to establish a dictatorial hold over the population, while another victory allowed him to have himself anointed and crowned king. He established what he imagined to be an Old Testament regime of splendour, with every luxury that the city could provide. The surplus of women was solved by the introduction of compulsory polygamy. Law and order disappeared, unless at the whim of King Jan. The strong abused the weak and full vent was given to all types of vice. When the city was at last taken, the besieging forces took great pleasure in hunting down and killing every survivor. It was almost a ritualistic cleansing after defilement. It was as if Anabaptism was a plague; all trace of it had to be burned out before people could feel relatively safe again.

For the rest of the century, mention of Münster was enough to provoke instant and unthinking hostility towards the religious radicals. Yet Anabaptists continued to win converts. In some areas, especially in the northern parts of the Netherlands, considerable numbers lived in relative tranquillity, thanks to the willingness of sympathetic local magistrates to turn a blind eye to them. But this only lasted as long as they kept themselves to themselves and did not antagonise their neighbours. It was by becoming almost invisible that Anabaptism survived. Those groups not swallowed up by the spread of Calvinism, in the second half of the century, ensured the continuation of their beliefs by exporting them to North America.

Tutorial

Summary of key ideas

Sola experientia (spiritualism) – salvation through internal religious experiences rather than through external free gifts of grace. Outward religious ceremonies are considered useless.

Radical Reformation

Three-fold baptism – the Anabaptist understanding of the importance of inner faith, consisting of inner baptism (recognition of grace and repentance), water baptism (a sign of faith and renewed life) and blood baptism or martyrdom (the expectation of worldly persecution).

Progress question
How were the Anabaptists the logical result of Zwinglian or Lutheran theology?

Seminar discussion
1. Why are the Anabaptists important to reformation studies?

2. Why were the Anabaptists left with such a bad reputation?

3. What do the Müntzer and Münster affairs tell us about social and political conditions in the early reformation period?

Practical assignment
You might encounter 'challenge statement' type questions (like 'The Anabaptists took Zwinglian doctrines to their logical conclusions.' Can this view be supported with reference to the Bible and sacraments?). This calls for a clear 'yes, for these reasons ...' or 'no, for these reasons ...' type answers. To prepare, list the possible answers and decide which is the better case.

Study and revision tips
1. You will almost certainly never be asked a question dealing with the Anabaptists alone (for lack of secondary source materials). Rather you will encounter compare/contrast type questions (with Luther or Zwingli). To prepare, make a chart of several columns, in which you can compare the beliefs, doctrines and influence(s) of these diverse beliefs.

2. Create a simple chart to help you visualise the specific issues at odds between the radicals and Luther or Zwingli or both.

6

Karlstadt

One minute summary – Karlstadt was a student of philosophy and theology, and a colleague of Luther's at Wittenberg. Karlstadt was at first influenced by Luther, but when he took over the reform movement at Wittenberg in his absence, he turned it in a new direction. He called on the city council to establish a 'new Jerusalem' by means of social changes (aimed at the poor) and religious changes (such as iconoclasm). Forced out on Luther's return, he developed his theories along interior, mystical lines, influencing the radicals. After the peasants' war, he fell under the influence of Zwingli and continued to develop his mystical doctrines. This chapter will help you to understand:

▶ why Karlstadt is an obscure but key figure
▶ the concept of proto-Puritanism
▶ Karlstadt's theologies in contrast to Luther's
▶ his doctrines of the eucharist, images and infant baptism
▶ the influence of Karlstadt on Müntzer.

Karlstadt: an obscure but key figure

Andreas Rudolf Bodenstein von Karlstadt (1480–1541) has remained an obscure figure largely as an accident of timing, and because of of his own temperament. Although he was a colleague and collaborator of Luther's, and accompanied him to his debate with Eck, he had great difficulties thinking on his feet. Karlstadt was bookish, and had little real practical experience of heated, fast-paced debate. For these reasons, little initial attention was paid to this bookworm, already overshadowed by his more famous friend. Later, after a career of accepting ever more obscure posts and of wandering the countryside, Karlstadt became influenced and overshadowed by Zwingli and the far more radical reform he seemed to inspire.

Karlstadt falls between these two greater personalities. You might legitimately ask, therefore, why give this man a chapter to himself? The answer lies in what Karlstadt represents, rather than in his second-ranked theological position. Karlstadt represents several ideals important for the reformation, including:

- ▶ practical church reform
- ▶ radical social reform
- ▶ the rejection of material, external justification, in favour of the internal, mystical regeneration of the individual

– all of which we will examine. While Luther was away from Wittenberg writing his theological treatises, and calling on the nobility to reform the church, Karlstadt was trying to tackle religious reform as an immediate practical issue, appealing to the common man to take up self-reform. Although this led to serious problems and a split between them, it was therefore Karlstadt – not Luther – who really launched the reformation.

The concept of 'proto-Puritanism'

On Luther's advice, or seeking to refute his anti-scholasticism, Karlstadt had carried out a painstaking examination of Augustinian primary sources. He then compared these with later scholastic theology. Karlstadt found himself agreeing with Luther against the near Pelagian reliance of the schoolmen on the human element in salvation, and their endless debates on useless matters. Karlstadt more or less echoed his mentor in denying human influence. Moreover, he agreed that the human will is passive, while God is active in granting grace.

For Luther, of course, this indicated that salvation was a force external to the recipient. Free grace is a favour God ascribes to sinners on their behalf, as he saw clearly emphasised in the gospels. This suggests that a person can be a sinner and righteous at the same time, without ever knowing (predestination). Karlstadt's reading of scripture and Augustine, however, led him to challenge this 'externalistic' view along Augustinian lines. Instead, he stressed an 'internalistic' view, with a more ethically based theology of regeneration, rather than accepting Luther's idea of free justification.

For Karlstadt, the scriptures were far more than the 'Word' of God merely instructing people in faith. They were divine laws governing both church and society, and ordering human behaviour along specific lines. God does not want man merely to believe. Rather, God wants man to *act*, to recognise his condition (sinfulness) and strive for inner righteousness, on the model of Old Testament biblical communities (obeying divine laws, etc.) and the model of Jesus himself. Karlstadt has thus been called the pioneer of Puritanism (hence the prefix *proto*), because his was a communal reform movement at the grass-roots level.

By the mid-1520s, Karlstadt had adopted the mystical theologies of the radicals much more fully, though he called for passive resistance rather than violent revolution. He also began to emphasise physical purgation as a means of experiencing Jesus's sufferings. In this way, the human will was to be subdued and subsumed by the divine (interior regeneration).

▶ *Picturing the scene* – You have probably seen comedy sketches in which monks knock themselves about with mortarboards or other more amusing objects (*Monty Python and the Holy Grail*). The serious intent behind such actions is that the pain experienced should remind the monk of Jesus's own suffering on mankind's behalf. The monk becomes closer to Jesus, and thus salvation, through shared experience.

Naturally, as Karlstadt developed his own interpretations of scripture, he began to challenge Luther's other sociological and theological interpretations as well.

Karlstadt's theologies contrasted with Luther's

Luther's interpretation of scripture led him to challenge Roman authority on several points. The most serious of these concerned the sacraments, salvation and church–state relations. It was on these issues that Luther and Karlstadt were most at odds. This is most evident in the 1521–2 period, during the so-called Wittenberg Disturbances, when Karlstadt was an active reformer at Wittenberg and Luther was in hiding at Wartburg.

Understanding Karlstadt's eucharistic theology

One of Karlstadt's earliest reforms was to celebrate the eucharist in both kinds. The student might think this was hardly new, as Luther supported the idea. The difference between them is interpretative, however. Karlstadt expresses the 'symbolic' understanding of the sacrament here for the first time. He attacked the doctrine of the *real presence* in the bread and wine, taking them rather as 'signs' of the spiritual presence of God, removing the perceived power of the material elements. This is naturally based on his reading of the relevant portions of scripture.

Where Jesus said 'this is my body', he did not mean – as Luther believed – that it was a real physical presence in the bread and the wine. Nor did he mean – as Zwingli believed – that he was symbolically present. For Karlstadt, the bread and the wine do not come into the equation at all; Jesus was pointing to himself and not the bread. (*John 6.63*: 'It is the spirit that gives life, the flesh is of no avail.')

Karlstadt made a key distinction between the flesh (real or symbolic) as represented by the bread eaten by the recipient, and the internal reception of Jesus through faith. In themselves, the bread and wine have no meaning.

Understanding the implications of this

Obviously, any new eucharistic theology would have drastic repercussions for the ceremony of the Mass which was the central act for thousands of people. Since the Mass was central to church services, any change would be deeply felt everywhere. Karlstadt stated clearly that for the communicant to take only the bread was itself a sin. It would be a rejection of internal regeneration, a rejection of faith itself.

In late December 1521, he made clear his intentions to institute a new Mass on 1st January, in line with his theology. Despite the orders of the elector not to proceed, Karlstadt revised his schedule and instituted the new Mass, without vestments, in German and in both kinds, on Christmas Day instead. This was a very public rejection both of tradition and of temporal authority in spiritual matters.

This is an interesting piece of history in itself, but there were wider implications. Karlstadt had clearly signalled to all where spiritual authority lay – in the hands of the common people. When Luther challenged the authority of Rome and its hierarchy, the question arose: who had the power to implement reform, was it the prince, the priest or the community?

1. Luther opted for the temporal power which, like his justification theology, again suggested externalistic reform.
   He believed the prince should reform the church on behalf of the people (the community).
2. Karlstadt opted for the community as a whole, consistent with his own theology of internal regeneration.

Karlstadt now began preaching in favour of iconoclasm, reminiscent of the eighth- and ninth-century image and idol-smashing movements in the Eastern Roman Empire. Iconoclasm would destroy the materialistic, externalised aspects of faith. He also proposed setting up a poor relief fund, with a new begging order, to help relieve social problems. Through his preaching, Karlstadt stirred up the common people to near-riot levels.

In an effort to prevent violence, or at least channel it, the Wittenberg town council began the wholesale implementation of his reforms. On 24th January, it backed his changes to the Mass, and his call for the removal of religious images. Other symbols of the Roman faith were treated with equal contempt, in a destruction of the material aspects of faith. Karlstadt called for still further reforms, but the elector stepped in to stop council action, and asked Karlstadt himself to stop preaching. Luther returned to help settle the town and took charge of the reform movement. Luther preached that Karlstadt had moved too far too fast, and criticised him for his focus on the common people. Luther called for a moderate, gradualist reform, which Karlstadt rejected.

▶ *Picturing the scene* – Think of yourself as a child playing with matches. Karlstadt claimed that by breaking your will and snatching away the matches at once (a short, sharp shock), he was acting in a brotherly, Christian fashion. Although you might cry for the loss of the matches, you could do yourself no more harm. Luther, or so it appears, would allow you to harm yourself with the fire, then remove the matches one by one, each removal giving you less chance of burning yourself. Thus, you would be gradually weaned off the matches without too much emotional distress.

Understanding Karlstadt's doctrine of baptism

Early on in his attempts at reform in Wittenberg, Karlstadt had stopped baptising infants for reasons similar to the Anabaptists'. His internalistic regeneration theory meant that man is saved (justified) through internal anguish. As with his doctrine on the eucharist, he distinguished between the act and what it symbolised.

Moreover, his refusal to baptise infants challenged social customs. Remember, for Luther, baptism represented the child's integration into the religious community as well as the acceptance of its political structure. Recall, too, that Zwingli retained infant baptism as a sign of the parents' willingness that the child should be a part of the community (a token of loyalty).

Leaving baptism until a person was adult indicated two things:

1. Karlstadt remained consistent with his internalistic approach. Only an adult could understand and articulate internal anguish, signalling his readiness to join the community.

2. Political freedom for the individual. Merely living in a particular town does not necessarily indicate obedience to its political and social powers. These powers might, in fact, be resisted.

Understanding the wider social and political implications

Karlstadt imagined an Old Testament 'apostolic' community. His attempts to bring about reforms in Wittenberg show his desire to make it a reality. Clearly, to carry it out, some disruption of the current socio-political order was necessary. He wanted the common people to grasp reform for themselves, though not necessarily by force. He wanted people to break their own 'self-will' so that it could be replaced by God's will.

Karlstadt offered himself up as an example. He reformed himself in several ways:

(a) He abandoned support of the papacy.
(b) He gave up his vow of celibacy by marrying a former nun.
(c) He encouraged the common people with drastic social reform.
(d) Over the following years, he resigned his archdiaconate, his university lectureship, his work as a parson and, finally, his work as a shopkeeper.

This last point is important as it shows the gradual lowering of his own social status in an effort to become closer to the common people (the poor), those at the heart of Jesus's message. In this way, he and everyone else could return to the idea of an 'apostolic church', a congregation with a heightened sense of lay piety (Puritanism), just as he had tried to turn Jesus's commandment of charity into a law. Just like the Anabaptists, he anticipated persecution, and possible martyrdom, although he usually fled town before that point. Interestingly, wherever he went he generally refused to discuss reform with city councillors, theologians or preachers. He turned instead to lay preachers as his target audience, those closest to ordinary people.

Karlstadt, Müntzer and the Peasants' War

It should be easy for you to anticipate how Karlstadt influenced the peasant uprisings of 1524–26. He was on the scene of one of the harshest theatres during the revolt, the small town of Rothenburg in Franconia where the townsfolk were in league with the peasants. Karlstadt later claimed that in May 1525 he had tried to mediate a peace between the peasants and townsfolk, and the ruling council. However, a cause and effect argument can be made since, after he fled, several of his townsfolk associates were executed.

In any case, it is clear that he had some influence over Müntzer, during his time of wandering Germany. He and Müntzer made contact through associates in Wittenberg, and Karlstadt helped Müntzer secure that preaching post in Allstedt and influenced his *sola experientia* theology.

Tutorial

Summary of key ideas
Proto-Puritanism – This term describes Karlstadt's attempts at reform in Wittenberg. These emphasised religious reform and socio-political change at the grass-roots level. Reform was to be carried out by the 'common man' for his own benefit. Proto-Puritanism involved an emphasis on lay preaching, the idea of creating an 'apostolic' religious community, and abandoning the old social and political divisions represented by the feudal class system.

Salvation through regeneration – For Karlstadt the key elements of salvation were change within the individual, experience of Jesus-like suffering, expression of internal anguish (recognition of sinfulness), and the desire for rebirth.

The eucharist – Karlstadt was the first to declare the merely symbolic nature of the ceremony. He denied the *real presence* of Jesus, and the importance of the bread and wine as anything other than signs of the recipient's recognition of faith through Jesus.

Progress questions
1. Explain the significance of salvation through regeneration and its wider social significance.

2. How does Karlstadt's eucharistic theology represent his internalistic approach to salvation?

3. Compare and contrast Luther's and Karlstadt's theologies.

Seminar discussion
1. Karlstadt was the 'theologian of the common man'. How valid

is this definition?

2. Did Karlstadt 'practise what he preached'? If so, how?

3. Why was Karlstadt an important reformation figure?

Practical assignment

You might well be asked a question on Karlstadt's impact on the reformation period. To prepare, try making a chart tracing his development from a Lutheran into a Zwinglian, and into a near-Anabaptist. Make notes explaining how he arrived at his final position.

Study and revision tips

To help you to understand the importance of Karlstadt's theologies, create a chart listing:

(a) in one column, the issues over which he and Luther disagreed
(b) in a second column, Luther's understandings
(c) in a third column, Karlstadt's understandings.

7

John Calvin

One minute summary – Jean Chauvin (1509–64), of Noyon in Picardy, was educated in Latin, Greek and law at the universities of Paris and Orléans. A brilliant scholar, he was also rigorously orthodox until, for reasons unknown, he became obsessed with Protestantism. Thereafter, he became a 'codifier'. He read the works of Erasmus, reworked the ideas and brought order and coherence to the doctrines of Luther and Zwingli – in short, he was less an original thinker and more an effective administrator. Calvin's travels took him to Basel, Strasbourg and Geneva while he developed his ideas, refined through continuous re-editing of his two works, *The Institutions of the Christian Religion* and *Reply to Sadoleto*. Although influenced by others, his importance rests on the fact that his writings challenged so many established assumptions and influenced so many beyond his immediate audience. Calvin dominated the second wave of reform. This chapter will help you to understand:

- the second wave of the Protestant reformation
- the doctrine of *double predestination*
- why Calvin rejected traditional salvation theory
- Calvin's reading of the sacraments
- Calvin's conception of the church *visible*
- the wider impact of Calvinism.

Calvin and the second wave of the reformation

Calvin has traditionally been presented as the man who brought order out of the chaos of the many confused doctrines of the 'first wave' reformations we have already examined. Valuable as this work was, however, he has not been seen as a very original thinker. This is due, perhaps, to three things:

1. misunderstanding of his central message (whether real or pretended)
2. re-formulation of his thinking by later adherents (his message was changed)
3. his willingness to admit he might be wrong.

Thus, he is thought of as an arranger or populariser of other men's thoughts and Protestant teachings. This is an error as Calvinism, sometimes called 'Reformed' religion, was unique in many ways:

(a) It challenged several basic assumptions about God and man.

(b) It had great political impact on developments in the Swiss Confederation.

(c) Where the Lutheran reformation was academic in context (Luther's examination and rejection of scholastic explanations), Calvinism originated in a series of moral reforms and modifications in worship (on a more biblical pattern).

(d) It was institutional, social and ethical (rather than religious).

(e) Calvin, himself, had relatively little deep interest in doctrine.

The term 'Calvinism'

Before we proceed, however, a word of caution. The term 'Calvinism' is often used interchangeably by older historians to refer to the religious ideas of the Reformed church as a whole. The student will find that more recent historians discourage this practice. Evidence increasingly suggests that later Reformed theologians drew on sources other than Calvin and, moreover, quietly altered his views to match and support theirs.

'Calvinist' is not a particularly safe term either. It dates from the Germany of the 1560s which, as we have seen, had been seriously destabilised by religious conflict between Lutherans and Catholics, at least up to 1555. Recall the famous principle *cuius regio, eius religio*. German territories had been divided between Lutherans and Catholics, but no provision had been made for the Reformed faith.

In February 1563, the *Heidelberg Catechism* was published, laying a claim for legitimacy for the Reformed church, but it was immediately attacked by Lutherans as 'Calvinist' or 'foreign' – in other words, disparagingly.

Importance of Calvinism in the English-speaking world

But, whichever term the student favours, it cannot be denied that of the three constituents of the Protestant reformation – Lutheran, radical or Calvinist – it is Calvinism which is of particular importance to the English-speaking world:

(a) In its Puritan form it figures highly in sixteenth- and seventeenth-century history.

(b) It was the intellectual explanation of the European and American witch hunts.

(c) It greatly influenced the religious and political views of the early Americans.

(d) It provided the underlying intellectual basis of black slavery.

For reasons of these repercussions alone, Calvinism needs to be examined and understood by history students.

Double predestination

We discussed common religious assumptions in Chapter 2. Like the Romans, Martin Luther and the humanists, Calvin agreed that God was the omnipotent, omniscient and omnipresent Creator of the universe, just and active in human affairs. For these others, however, God is also love, at which point Calvin parts company.

▶ *You are there* – To understand why, imagine yourself living at the time. Illness could strike at any time, there were no warnings of natural disasters, physical abuse was common. In other words, life was hard and held cheap. There was no concept of basic human rights. Would you have agreed with Calvin that God was more interested in final justice than in love?

God, for Calvin, was responsible for everything that happened in the world but, as bad as this might seem, he held that man (evil and trivial) deserved no better.

▶ *Picturing the scene* – We have all seen police dramas wherein some criminal is punished for a crime which we later discover he did not commit. Some wag always dismisses the mistake because he was no doubt 'guilty of something'. This was how Calvin saw the kinship between God and man. Since God is just, He would not punish the innocent but, since trials and tribulations are common, humans must all be 'guilty of something'.

For Calvin, God was to man as man is to the ant – beneath notice. Like a slave, the point of human existence was to meet God's demands unquestioningly.

Calvin's doctrine of predestination

Predestination has come to be seen as the central focus of Calvin's work. This is a mistake, however, perpetuated by enemies who failed to understand him. Calvin himself puzzled over the fuss caused by such a minor and rather obvious aspect of his thinking.

He started with the basic assumptions (Chapter 2). An allknowing, all-powerful God *must* pre-destine and pre-know all the actions and all the thoughts of everyone since creation. In itself, this appears a logical assumption. Combined with his assumptions about man, however, such thinking had serious implications for human salvation. Remember, for the Catholics and Luther, salvation depended on the actions of the individual (do good works or simply believe). But, can the actions of the individual ant stop traffic? God had willed a man's fate, saved or damned, at the beginning of time; surely nothing could now be done about it? In this, Calvin also challenged the medieval concept of free will.

An early medieval argument was being echoed. It was a paradox to hold that man was free to choose or reject God, yet acknowledge

God as omnipotent and omniscient. Erasmus argued for the existence of free will as a kind of human right to accept or reject saving grace, allowed by a loving God.

▶ *Picturing the scene* – Erasmus is saying that you have been given free will to believe what you will and act as you like, as a kind of divine test. In the end, the just God will judge you fairly and, based on your life, you will enter hell or heaven.

Traditional theories of free will have a kind of simple, attractive logic about them. It made great sense but still there was that element of human influence on God which Calvin found absurd. Oddly, he did not deny free will. The ant could certainly *try* to stop traffic. Calvin's explanation of how he was not denying it, however, is far too subtle for even the best educated academic theologians, so we will leave it alone. Except for this theological imbroglio, Calvin was generally agreeing with most others.

The omniscient God was, of course, already well aware of the decisions that men would make in their lifetimes.

▶ *Single predestination*, the generally held belief, stated that God 'predicted', from the time of creation, whether an individual would be saved or damned, opting to explain that, really, only the elect where predestined for salvation. Calvin took this one step further.

▶ *Double predestination* held that, of course, God knew from creation who was to be saved or damned (it was not a prediction) as a positive decision. In other words, God created good and evil, blessed the good and cursed the evil and, in fact, predestined who would be good and who would be evil. Certainly it was not for the mind of mortals to comprehend God's purposes. Obviously, his *double predestination* doctrine was highly influential on his salvation theology.

Calvin's theology of salvation

We have discussed several salvation doctrines and their differences already. In one way, however, all the previous reformers and the traditionalists had something in common. All tried to formulate an understudying of human salvation which did not hold God responsible for evil – be it free will, original sin, human weaknesses, disease, subtle shades of predestination meanings. All these ideas still indicated that man had some influence. Calvin would have none of this. Given his assumptions about God, mankind and predestination, how could he possibly have thought otherwise?

For Calvin, an individual was either elect or reprobate (damned) – end of story. Moreover, while Luther, Zwingli and even the radicals hinted that the elect could recognise themselves, Calvin was having none of that either. It was impossible to tell, although all would be revealed after death. Calvin would relent somewhat on this harsh stance later and allow that persecution for your beliefs *might* be a token of salvation.

Understanding the implications

If you could do nothing about it, why not adopt a fatalistic attitude and live life any way your fancy took you? Such thinking was a problem for Calvin. He wanted people to seek divine grace by living a good life, performing good deeds and acts of charity, but he did not want them to assume these had merit in the eyes of God. Moreover, he was unwilling to allow that those who considered themselves damned should have that *carte blache* to sin without personal blame. God might not be loving, but He was just, so Calvin held that there was a 'hidden equity' behind God's decisions somewhere.

This might appear to you as a rather artificial answer and, indeed, it was. For Calvin, unlike the others, there was really little point in dwelling on a matter ineffable to the human mind and unchangeable by human will. It might be difficult for you (it was for early modern theologians) to reconcile the idea that God is just and equitable with the idea that a sinful, otherwise evil man could be elect and the good, saintly man could be damned.

To explain away the inconsistency, much like the others, Calvin turned to the place of Jesus in theology. Jesus was sacrificed for the sins of mankind. Therefore, the elect were justified in the eyes of God

– pretty basic and understandable reasoning. There is, however, a self-created difficulty with which Calvin, alone among the reformers, had to deal. A 'loving' God might well sacrifice His divine, perfect son for the sake of all mankind, but would a 'just' God have done so for the sake of a mankind beneath His notice? Calvin approached this question two ways. Either through circular logic – 'a just God could not act in an unjust manner so, though mortal man might not understand it, the sacrifice of Jesus was just' – or, by dividing Jesus's nature into its divine (perfect) and human (flawed) constituencies. By punishing Jesus's human nature, not his divine nature, God was just.

You might well smirk at what must appear to be pretty flimsy reasoning. Of all the reformers we have examined, Calvin was the most likely to agree that it was flimsy, but he was also the first to admit that he did not have all the answers. We have all heard the expression 'God only knows'; Calvin appealed to this cliché again and again as a good, albeit unsatisfying, explanation.

Calvin's doctrine of the sacraments

Like both the traditionalists and the major reformation thinkers, Calvin attached great importance to the sacraments (rejecting them as vehicles of grace, however). Like his Protestant colleagues, he also rejected the traditional view of seven sacraments. He was willing to accept only the eucharist and baptism. He placed a high spiritual value on these two, however, as physical representations of man's desire to draw closer to Jesus and, therefore, held the eucharist (or Lord's Supper) as a vital part of worship, however out of step he was with his Genevan audience.

He disagreed with Luther, however, over the idea of the *real presence*. He reasoned that, as Jesus was in heaven, seated on the right side of God, he could not also be in the bread. This is representative of a very subtle dispute over the two natures of Jesus which we will not pursue here. Suffice it to say that Jesus's physical body could not be in more than one place at any one time.

Calvin also disagreed with Zwingli, however, over his view of the wine and bread as symbolic representations. Calvin looked to spiritual meanings. Jesus was present in a 'spiritual' way, and given to the recipients in the bread and wine, spiritually. The Holy Spirit made the sacrament important, leading the recipients to Jesus. Because of the presence of the Holy Spirit, Calvin also insisted that children be publicly baptised at the first opportunity, else their presence would be a stain on the church *visible*. Ultimately, it must be said, he was unconcerned precisely how Jesus was present, and warned his followers to embrace the mystery rather than try to puzzle it out.

The church 'visible'

Above, we said that an unbaptised child would, in Calvin's view, be a stain on the church *visible*, which needs further explanation. We have already examined the question of what the church was, so the basic concepts of church *visible* and *invisible* are already familiar. To briefly recap:

▶ The church *visible* means the gathering of all professed believers.

▶ The church *invisible* is the elect amongst them.

We have also examined various understandings of what the true church was and was not. Like the other thinkers, Calvin held that the true church based its teachings purely on scripture and celebrated the sacraments in a pure manner. (Note: he was willing to accept that his own Biblical interpretation was but one of many, and so had no difficulty in accepting the validity of Luther's or Zwingli's interpretations.)

The distinction between the reformers is two-fold. First, how was membership of the church *invisible* gained? In brief:

(a) for traditionalists, through good works
(b) for Luther, through faith alone
(c) for Karlstadt, through self-recognition
(d) for Anabaptists, through interior mystical experiences.

In other words, membership was gained via salvation. Calvin

agreed with none of these methods, of course, because he thought of salvation in a different way. He held that membership in the church *invisible* was (like salvation) through divine election from the time of creation. This being the case, discussion was pointless. Calvin opted to examine membership in the church *visible* instead.

Calvin's emphasis on the church *visible*

Still, Calvin had much in common with the other major reformers over this question too. He, like they, wanted everybody within the local political unit included for practical and obvious reasons of social stability. He, like they, believed that the political or temporal authorities had a voice in the church *visible*, and they all rejected the Roman hierarchy of pope, bishops and priests. In fact, Calvin modelled the Genevan church on Bucer's work in Strasbourg.

For Calvin, like the humanist urban reformers, the spiritual and temporal worked side by side with an equal voice. In practical detail, Calvin – with the town council – established the consistory, the highest church disciplinary body. This was made up of ministers (in the minority) and elders (lay men in the majority). The actual service was, as elsewhere, carried out by doctors and deacons (teachers and administrators) very much like Luther's own ministers. In one aspect, however, Calvin's thinking on the church visible was unique.

For the other major reformation thinkers, and indeed, for the Romans, the church visible was important because it offered those things necessary for human salvation, and because it cemented the community together. No one in the community should be allowed to turn their back on the local church (*cuius regio, eius religio*). The Anabaptists were universally feared and hated for having done just this, and those who persisted in ignoring the local church were often branded and burned as heretics. In the spirit of co-operation, priests identified the culprits and the temporal powers executed them. These other thinkers, however, considered the church visible as something set up for the benefit of the individual or for that of the community. It was there to meet their needs.

Calvin saw the church visible in an entirely different light. It was set up for the benefit of God. It was there to serve God's will, not man's. This being the case, he insisted that those who were clearly unworthy, and those who did not want to attend, be positively excluded so as not to stain what belonged to God.

The impact of Calvinism

You might well ask why Calvinism had the impact it did? What does he offer which Luther or Karlstadt do not? The answer to this is only partially religious and, perhaps, less religious than we might expect. Much of the wider impact of Calvin's doctrine, in fact, is based on underlying political and geographical causes.

Understanding the geo-political causes

Calvin was French by birth and had never lost interest in the affairs of his native lands. Nor was this too difficult. Geneva was geographically surrounded by France after 1536, when the duchy of Savoy was annexed by Francis I. Long-suffering French Protestants often took refuge from the latest persecutions in this city and, from about 1541, Calvin began translating his major works into French for export.

In actual fact, though, Calvin did not agitate his French contacts for religious rebellion. He had too much on his plate in Geneva to involve himself in other men's affairs. Of course, the French government would have cracked down very harshly indeed on such a movement, and Calvin was never inclined to support underground movements anyway. His attitude changed in 1554 when he began supporting and advising French congregations and organising Reformed churches. What had changed was that, by this time, a great percentage of the noble classes of Southern France were also converting. Thus, real political success was possible. 'Huguenot' churches became very significant, and Geneva trained and dispatched upwards of ninety ministers to aid them.

Clearly, Calvinism had appeal to French-speaking peoples, written, as it was, in French by a Frenchman. It also spread outside the francophone world. It reached other parts of Switzerland, Holland, England, Scotland, Poland and Hungary, and eventually America, though it made few inroads into German-dominated areas, even after the spread of Lutheranism slowed.

John Calvin

Nationalism

Historians offer up many theories to explain this but, more than likely, nationalism is the answer. Where German was the 'elite' language, where the Empire was politically dominant, adopting Calvinism as the model of religious reform became a kind of signal of dissent and expression of ethnic assertiveness. This, combined with the fact that French was rapidly overtaking Latin as the language of culture, law and diplomacy, made books written in French seriously in demand. No single explanation is completely satisfactory, of course, and you should remain open-minded.

Tutorial

Summary of key ideas

Salvation – Humans were either saved or damned at the moment of creation and, consequently, can do absolutely nothing to influence God's choices.

Double predestination – All agreed that God was omniscient and omnipotent and that the 'elect' were predestined for salvation, but only Calvin stressed that God had made a positive decision to predestine the 'reprobate' for damnation as well.

Church visible – It was generally agreed that the visible church encompassed all members of the local community, but Calvin stressed that those considered unworthy should be excluded because the church was created for the benefit of God and not the benefit of man. The presence of the unworthy was, therefore, a stain.

The eucharist – This is a true sacrament which provided no grace, no miracles, with no *real presence* or symbolic presence, but with a spiritual presence of Jesus through the Holy Spirit.

Progress questions

1. Explain how Calvin's understanding of human salvation differs from that of every other major reformation thinker. Give examples.

2. Summarise how Calvin's thoughts on the nature of God and man influenced his theology.

3. How is Calvinism not merely the amalgamation of earlier Protestant types? Give examples.

Seminar discussion
1. How can the success and spread of Calvinism, or Reformed religion, best be explained?

2. Had you been alive at that time, how would Calvinism have made a difference in your own life? If you had been French? Genevan? German?

Practical assignment
Through further readings, trace the spread of Calvinism from Geneva outwards. Take note of other Reformed groups (Huguenots, Puritans, Presbyterians, Anglicans) and chart how they have adapted Calvinist beliefs to their own usage.

Study and revision tips
1. List any difficulties you have had with Calvin's doctrines. Make further readings on these topics and ask your tutor for guidance.

2. Make a chart of all Calvin's basic theological positions and compare them with those of Luther and Zwingli. Make a list of the major disagreements and the reasons for them.

8

The Catholic Reformation

One minute summary – What we will call the Catholic reformation is actually an amalgam of two distinct historical 'events'. The first is the traditionally regarded 'Catholic reformation', which pre-dates Luther and actually developed for much the same reasons as Lutheranism. This was a revival of religious practices, as understood by doctrinal orthodoxy. It took place either through reform of the hierarchy, regular religious groups and lay fraternities, or through more rigorous enforcement methods. It was, in many ways, the natural evolution of Catholicism as a result of scholasticism, humanism and rising lay expectations. The second event is the so-called 'counter-reformation', which is how Protestant historians tend to label the Catholic response to the issues raised by the Protestants. Reformers expressed the great need to define and clarify doctrinal issues exclusive of what they saw as Protestant innovation. This chapter will help you to understand:

▶ pre-Lutheran Catholic reform movements
▶ the need for new lay fraternities and monastic orders, and the response
▶ the importance of the Jesuits
▶ why the papacy could not reform itself
▶ the intended and actual use of the Index and the Inquisition
▶ the work of the Council of Trent

Pre-Lutheran Catholic reform movements

Long before Martin Luther, the need for reform, particularly in Rome itself, was widely recognised. Savonarola (1452–98), for example, died a heretic for his reform efforts in Florence. Equally, in Spain, biblical revision and translation was being carried out long before Erasmus produced his *Greek New Testament*. As we have discussed, the reformers were responding to lay expectations and, in particular, to humanism's emphasis on the individual and personal religious experience.

Understanding the new orders

We have noted the rising tide of anti-monastic criticism. New monastic orders were founded to try and avoid the spiritual decay seen elsewhere. Ignatius Loyola (1491–1556), for example, founded the Society of Jesus, and others inspired new orders which reflected rising popular piety. Among them were the:

▶ Capuchins
▶ Oratories of Divine Love
▶ Ursulines
▶ Theatines.

In brief, such foundations were meant to increase both the morale and spirituality of believers, and give those with heightened mystical interests a chance to express them in positive ways. These groups embodied 'activism in grace'. This was divine grace expressed through a subdued and disciplined will, and in works of charity and social service. Obviously, the human element in salvation was still recognised.

The Capuchins
Moreover, all groups found some representation. The Capuchins, for instance, were a group of friars who split off from their Franciscan brethren in order better to express their views on the relationship of God and man. They aimed to combine poverty and material self-denial with works on behalf of the poor and indigent. As true hermits, they preached and tended to others' material needs; they ignored academic study in favour of spiritual contemplation in isolation.

Oratories
The lay need for spiritual expression was satisfied by the many Oratories founded throughout Italy in the early 1510s. These orders

The Catholic Reformation

were purpose-built for laymen who shared with ordained priests a spiritual desire for self-improvement and works of charity, but who did not want to give up their temporal lives. The members met regularly for contemplation, worship, study, and to perform acts of charity. The spiritual revival of the friars and laymen are evidenced by such groups.

The Theatines

Priests, too, were looking to express a new commitment to spiritual growth. They found expression in the new Theatine order. Made up exclusively of noble-born priests, their co-founders were Thomas de Vio (Cajetan) whom we have already encountered, and Giovanni Carafa (1476–1559), who later became Pope Paul IV (future organiser of the Roman Inquisition). In essence, the Theatines set a new standard of priestly practice and commitment.

The Ursulines

The most interesting of the new orders was undoubtedly the Ursulines, the most famous of the exclusively female orders, based on the Oratories. They were originally envisioned as regular and organised meetings of unmarried women to carry out works of charity, visit the sick and give religious instruction to women outside the usual formal structures. Originally, these groups also carried on 'normal' lives. This came to be seen as an innovation too far, however, and they were eventually restructured as a traditional enclosed order of nuns with the normal vows of poverty, chastity and obedience.

▶ *You are there* – Imagine yourself as an unmarried girl living in early modern Italy. You 'officially' had little or no independent legal status. You were *either* someone's daughter, sister, wife, *or* you were a nun (a 'bride of Christ') and dead to the outside world. The more superstitious would view you with suspicion for being of both worlds (but wholly of neither) and church officials would be uncomfortable with your freedom from the usual religious strictures.

For all of the good these new orders inspired, the history student must be cautioned against over-emphasising them. Little historical work has been carried out on the wider impact of such groups, and little written about similar groups originating outside Italy, with the great exception of the Jesuits. Use these groups as examples of rising levels of piety, expectation, charitable organisation, and awakening of the need for reform, rather than as innovative reform movements in themselves. You will most often encounter the new orders, anyway, as background detail for, or as precursors of, the Jesuits.

The Jesuits: Ignatius Loyola and Francis Xavier

Iñigo López de Recalde (1491–1556), better known as Ignatius Loyola, and Francis Xavier (1506–1622) founded the Compaña de Jesu, or Society of Jesus. It received papal approval in 1540 to undertake pilgrimages to the Holy Land – Palestine – and convert Muslims. However, this purpose was pre-empted by the Turkish-Venetian war, so Loyola re-dedicated the order to his own unique ideals of monasticism, similar to the orders above, and as reflected in his two great works, *Spiritual Exercises* and *Constitutions*.

Loyola replaced the old ideas of isolated contemplation and withdrawal from material existence with the need to act within material society. Essentially, he wanted men to strive for salvation through good works and charity, and to develop their individual spirituality and morale. At the same time, they should preach the traditional doctrines and beliefs of the church. This required well-educated, well-motivated priests dedicated to the ultimate authority of the pope as the vicar of God.

▶ *Key point* – Loyola and the Jesuits viewed the hierarchical structure of the church as not only right, but of supreme importance.

▶ *Picturing the scene* – Imagine yourself as a Jesuit. The church hierarchy, ruled by the pope, was established by God through the Holy Spirit, which infuses every level. To be effective, your self-discipline must be such that, if the pope rules that white is now black or day is now night, you will believe it so and teach it to others with complete sincerity. Could you be that dedicated?

The Jesuits were of course also committed to bringing the Protestants back into the traditional fold. They aimed to do this by:

(a) re-education
(b) propagation of traditional Christianity abroad (to prevent the spread of heresy)
(c) political influence at the highest levels
(d) underground missionary work in Protestant lands.

Papal reform

The great question which perplexes most students is why the papacy could not reform itself when reform was so clearly needed? This requires a subtle answer. Much lip service was paid to the idea of papal reform, and it cannot be denied that the desire for it and recognition of the need was there. Yet, as we have discussed, popes of the early period fell rather short on spirituality. Lest we judge too harshly, international politics was of greater concern because the popes were trying to avoid being swallowed up by France or by the Habsburgs. The popes required political autonomy in order to focus on spiritual matters.

In 1522, it looked as if reform was on the cards. Adrian of Utrecht, a deeply spiritual man, had been elected Pope Adrian VI and readily admitted to the problems in the Church. Alas, he lasted only eighteen months. In 1523, Guilio de'Medici was elected as Clement VII, and a traditional political-type pope was he. Yet in an odd sort of way, it was because of his overt political interests that the long-standing voices in favour of reform were finally heard. He tried to break Rome free of subservience to the Empire by throwing his support behind France, hoping to balance foreign power in Italy.

At Pavia in 1525, however, Emperor Charles V destroyed the French army and captured Francis I and, as he was unable to pay his army, looked the other way as they took out their spite on a virtually defenceless Rome. If nothing else, a clear message was sent. No papal opposition to the emperor's policies would be tolerated. Of course, the more spiritually minded saw this as God's wrath for the impure nature of their Church. The weak-willed Clement prevaricated until he was succeeded in 1534 by Alexander Farnese. Pope Paul III (1534–49) was certainly better suited to reform. He possessed a genuine desire to correct abuses and increase spiritual vigour among the clergy. He set up a reform committee of nine trusted cardinals, including Gasparo Contarini (a liberal) and Gian Pietro Carafa (a conservative). The committee worked for about nine months in 1536 and prepared a sweeping report calling for several institutional changes, including:

1. the papacy giving up the selling of exemptions
2. the papacy no longer selling positions in the Church
3. the bishops to be resident in their dioceses (thus, none could be cardinals).

These recommendations would have brought a storm of protest and short-term financial ruin, so Paul could only accept them 'in principle' and refused to authorise publication (although Contarini published it in 1538 without permission, to the delight of the Lutherans). For all this, the pope did authorise the single most important recommendation – to summon a general council. This became the Council of Trent (see below).

So, while the need for reform was self-evident, the popes were caught on the horns of a dilemma: go the way of the liberals and risk too much Protestant-looking change, or go the way of the conservatives and risk alienating more people. By 1541 Paul was pushed to the conservatives by reports of the growing numbers of Lutherans in northern Italian cities. The eventual solutions, besides Trent, were the **Index** and the **Inquisition**.

The Index of Prohibited Books

The Index of Prohibited Books was a censorship measure, combining a number of smaller prohibited book lists promulgated by the Catholic universities. It was really an exercise in thought control. Burning the authors and their books was not enough; possession had to equate with heresy too. Unfortunately, the Index was not limited to books long held to be heretical – anything by Luther, for instance. It included humanist classics such as the works of Erasmus, unauthorised vernacular Bible translations, and

The Catholic Reformation

editions of the church Fathers. You may well boggle at the cultural implications this had for Italian literature and art.

Later, with Calvinism spreading into hitherto Protestant-free zones, the duties of the Index were transferred to the Holy Office. This resulted in the suppression of cultural innovations in many Catholic countries in Europe and further afield well into the twentieth century.

Understanding the Inquisition

You will undoubtedly know about the 'Spanish' Inquisition – a rich source of humour for Mel Brooks and Monty Python – but many of the popular impressions are false. In Spain, the Inquisition had been re-established after the old thirteenth-century model. It was a crown court with overriding powers to investigate all accusations of heresy, but it was hardly the early KGB, Gestapo or CIA it is often made out to be. It did inspire fear, certainly, but this was the result of good publicity rather than actual torture. Historians now know that the punishments were less severe than previously thought, but also that the inquisitors themselves were far better orators and actors. The major weapon of the inquisitors was less the rack and more the stage – heretics and recanters were 'publicly' shamed.

> ▶ *Picturing the scene* – Today, when the phrase 'all publicity is good publicity' is regularly quoted, the student might have difficulty with the idea of shame as a powerful weapon. Recall that sixteenth-century society was tribal in nature, one in which social cliques were very important. What would your own life be like if no one looked at you, spoke to you, or dealt with you in any way, for fear of your shame rubbing off on them? Now, intensify that feeling ten-fold and throw in the wrath of God for good measure. Would you want to face the Inquisition? What would you do to avoid it?

This is not to deny that torture was used. Of course it was, but it was an accepted practice then and would have raised no eyebrows. Indeed, by this time, the health risks of torture were being recognised and taken into account. Nor were trials carried out in public.

The names of those accused, the accusers and all witnesses were kept secret to protect the innocent (to a degree which modern justice entirely fails to match). It is the judgement of many historians that the idea of a 'fair trial', which exists now only in theory, was the *modus operandi* of the Inquisition. It worked so well in Spain that, in July 1542, a similar organisation was re-established in Rome in an attempt to curb the growth of Protestantism in Italy. This was the Supreme Sacred Congregation of the Holy Office, which is referred to today by historians under the title 'Holy Office'. Where the Jesuits were the offensive weapons of the church, the Inquisition was the defensive weapon (Linberg, p.345).

The Council of Trent

A general council of the church was assembled so that doctrinal ambiguities, so well exploited by the Protestants, could be clarified and settled. Reconciliation with the Protestants was recognised as a mere pipe-dream, so another goal was the prevention of further loss, by strengthening the faith in established Catholic areas. An effort of self-renewal was also made whereby traditions were affirmed and papal authority recognised. You might well ask, however, why it took so long to summon it?

Background difficulties to a council

There were any number of problems with which to deal before a council could have been summoned. These included:

(a) politics
(b) authority
(c) choice of location
(d) procedural difficulties.

The pope could summon a general council at any time, but it was well within the power of local rulers to effectively veto it. For example, they could prevent the summons being circulated in their territories, and stop clergymen from travelling out. Should a council be successfully convened, however, it might become a focal point of papist-conciliarist tensions rather than a forum of doctrinal discussion.

The Catholic Reformation

On the matter of location, a council could not proceed without the co-operation of Charles V and Francis I. But hold the council in France, for example, and the emperor would veto it in favour of a location in Germany or Spain (which Francis would veto). As neither would welcome a council in the papal states, it took a while to agree on the least bad location, which was Trent. Even so, voting, proxies, meeting times and the agenda for discussions had still to be ironed out.

The council was eventually summoned by Paul III and met in three distinct periods between December 1545 and December 1563. Over these eighteen years, meetings were held in twenty-seven sessions of varying length. The basic details are these:

▶ The first period, December 1545 to September 1549 (although actually suspended in 1547), was divided into ten sessions examining definitions of church teachings.

▶ The second period, May 1551 to April 1552, was divided into six sessions examining definitions of faith.

▶ The third period, January 1562 to December 1563, was divided into eleven sessions examining definitions of faith and church discipline.

▶ 270 bishops attended at one time or another. They included 187 Italians, 31 Spanish (Iberian), 26 French, 2 Germans, 10 from the Balkans, 3 each from Portugal and Ireland, 2 each from Holland, Poland and Hungary, one Englishman and one Moravian (Greengrass, p.207).

Although great, the Italian numbers are not evidence of papal domination. The bishops of southern Italy (under Habsburg rule) and those of Venice were certainly not papacy-oriented and, in any case, there were at least four different schools of thought in evidence among them, split along religious lines. These were:

1. the *spirituali*, who emphasised the role of the visible church

2. the Augustinians, who questioned human effort in salvation

3. the Duns Scotus group, which limited the role of human effort in salvation (this included the Franciscans)

4. the Thomists, who believed in the human effort and the effectiveness of good works (this included the Dominicans)

Moreover, each bishop had a unique view; no pope ever visited the council, and his legates adopted a position as neutral chairmen (Davidson, p.10).

Results of the Council of Trent

What conclusions can be reached? It was most important to the bishops that clear lines of demarcation be drawn between orthodoxy and Protestantism. You should already know what the major issues were, so let us examine the Trent response.

One major issue was the source of doctrinal authority. Most Protestants favoured *sola scriptura* while Catholics held a special regard for written and unwritten traditions and the church Fathers. The gathered bishops wondered, though, whether the Bible and tradition were not of equal weight as sources of revelation. It was concluded that the teaching authority of the Roman church was the final judge of both (recall Luther's questioning of papal authority). They also decided that the *Vulgate*, despite its obvious translation errors, was the best source of scriptural evidence, humanist scholarship notwithstanding, although reading vernacular translations was not banned.

The second major contested issue was the Protestant doctrine of *justification by faith alone*. Catholics claimed that humans had a clear co-operative role and influence over God's decisions of election or damnation. The basic issue here was the point of Christian life. As we have seen, much church dogma depended on the efficacy of good works, but it was the aspect of saving grace which gave special significance to the sacraments, the veneration of saints, pilgrimages, joining a religious order and performing charitable deeds. If man could not influence salvation by his own efforts, then what was the point of any religious activity?

The discussion of justification and salvation spanned the most sessions and produced the longest set of statements, but on other doctrinal questions, the council was equally decisive:

The Catholic Reformation

(a) The traditional five-part view of salvation was re-affirmed.
(b) Traditional teachings on original sin were accepted.
(c) All seven sacraments were recognised as vehicles of divine grace.
(d) *Transubstantiation* was the true explanation of the *real presence*.
(e) Communion in one kind only (the bread for the laity) was accepted as legitimate.

Doctrinal issues were largely settled in the first two periods. The third was able to concentrate on matters of hierarchy and discipline.

Protestants, in general, had taken a stand against the traditional Roman hierarchy in favour of more locally or theologically suitable models. In effect, they elevated and emphasised the role of the individual at the expense of the clergy, encouraging people to form their own opinions by careful and sincere study of the Bible. In response, the councillors decreed that:

▶ The interpretation of scripture was not an appropriate activity for the individual church member.

▶ Men in orders were set apart and above other men.

▶ No one could interpret scripture other than the teaching authority of the Church (essentially, the pope).

In essence, the 'priesthood of all believers' was denied. These issues, of course, are basically doctrinal and reasonably safe points of debate. Questions of administration and political authority within the church, however, were less safe as these raised strong emotions of nationalistic or personal natures.

Certainly, the various Protestant groups had raised some legitimate concerns over the unchecked powers of the pope and the higher clergy. What emerged was a struggle between:

(a) those who saw that reforms would lead to material and political disadvantages (in the short term) with a corresponding effect on discipline

(b) those who believed that changes were necessary and could even result in a spiritually revitalised church (in the long run).

Administrative reforms

In the end, administrative reforms were made, but in such a way as to limit any threat to the power of the papacy or to the diocesan authority of the bishops. Some good reforms, in theory, were decreed. These include enactments on episcopal responsibility. Bishops must:

- set a sound example by leaving aside the pursuit of personal or familial enrichment, visit all their parishes, study the work of their priests, discipline their underlings and watch out for signs of heresy

- decline offers of money (beyond fixed assessments) or gifts (except for food during visitations)

- make up any shortfall of priests by doing the work themselves (regular preaching, administering the sacraments) and found a seminaries to train new priests

- live exclusively in their diocese and hold no other offices

- meet certain minimal qualifications – be of legitimate birth, a certain age, well educated in theology or law, and ordained no less than six months prior to their elevation.

Although their diocesan authority was recognised, how was it to be enforced? The existence of legal loop-holes, papal exemptions and lay patronage often undermined the bishops' intentions. To combat this, it was decided that exemptions would no longer apply to any clerical post that involved a cure of souls, and a decision was made to empower bishops to veto the appointment of any priest to such a post (including the regulars). As a guideline, all priests must:

(a) have good service records
(b) be at least twenty-five years old
(c) have spent at least one year as deacons prior to ordination
(d) have sufficient learning and sound morals, that is, be able to preach once a week and every feast day and teach the basics of the faith.

The Catholic Reformation

There were to be no further question marks over the competence and moral standard of the Roman clergy and, over time, their image did improve.

Tutorial

Summary of key ideas

Catholic/counter-reformation – These are two historically opposed explanations for the reform of the Roman Catholic church during the reformation, in which reform is seen as either an ongoing evolutionary process or as a response to Protestant gains.

Jesuits – The most important new order of the Catholic church dedicated to the service of the pope and the combat of Protestantism through education and political influence.

Index (the) – Created about 1571 to provide censorship and to condemn 'heretical' books and, later, other art forms which it considered dangerous to Catholic morality and to the faith.

Inquisition (the) – An ecclesiastical tribunal (in Spain under the crown's authority) established to investigate and suppress heresy and heretical opinions.

Progress questions
1. Explain why papal reform took so long to achieve.

2. Do the new orders prove the rise of lay piety and expectations? If so, are they an adequate response? If not, how best to explain their development? Give examples.

3. Assess how far the Council of Trent achieved its goals.

Seminar discussion
1. Which is the better description of events in the 1500–1570 period, Catholic reformation or counter-reformation?

2. Which had the greater impact on living Catholics, Trent or the rise of the Jesuits?

Practical assignment
Through further readings, trace the results of the Catholic reform movements. Take note of the influence of the Roman Catholic church outside Europe and of any problems encountered (like Jansenism).

Study and revision tips
1. List the major differences between the Catholics and the various Protestants with a brief note explaining these differences. Make further readings on these topics and ask your tutor for guidance.

2. Make a chart of two columns divided between counter and Catholic reformation statements. List examples under each column (with a brief explanatory note as to why you placed each example where you did).

Conclusion

One minute summary – The reformation, as a series of religiously motivated movements, influenced ways of thinking in the period and was, consequently, both a success and a failure. It was a success in that doctrinal, social and political changes were inspired and carried out, and in that Europe was irreconcilably divided along religious lines. It was a failure in that many of its various objectives were either never achieved, were found to be at loggerheads with other objectives or were only ever short-term and superficial in the first place (that is, change in name only). This conclusion will help you to understand:

▶ the reformation as intellectual change
▶ the reformation as cultural change
▶ the importance of the Thirty Years War.

The impact of the European reformation

Assessing the reformation in intellectual, social or political terms is, perhaps, the most difficult task the student will ever be assigned. This book gives the student the basic facts but, even so, with their greater command of the details, familiarity with the intricacies and years more experience, professional historians still argue over the reformation's real impact. As our purpose was to provide a reasonable start and a basic knowledge of the subject, here we will consider only the essentials. Historians, on both sides, use three basic criteria in making their assessments:

1. doctrine
2. social change
3. political power.

Understanding how the reformation succeeded
From a (Protestant) doctrinal point of view, the reformation succeeded in a number of ways, including:

- a triumphant challenge to papal authority
- the replacement of the Mass by the sermon as the central focus
- the Mass, in both kinds and in the local vernacular, was no longer a sacrificial service
- authority now centralised in the Bible (available in the vernacular)
- the undermining of scholastic theology.

It can certainly not be denied that three new religious communities had resulted, while for the Roman Catholics, doctrine was clarified and strengthened and intellectual bulwarks were raised against the Protestants. The reformation also succeeded from a social point of view and in a number of important ways. Key among these gains were:

- the destruction of clerical elitism in Protestant areas
- the recognition of social equality
- enhancement of the status of women
- more emphasis on education and the foundation of new schools
- the normalisation of language and new regard for literature, art and music (in Lutheran areas).

Indeed, from a cultural-social point of view, because of doctrinal reform almost all social activities were embellished with spiritual significance. Because all believers were equal, the baker was as important as the bishop.

It is vitally important that the student remember that all believers were considered as equal parts of the community. Therefore, bringing new members into the community was at least as important as offering services to the existing membership. In this way, parenthood, marriage, a new appreciation of 'gender' roles and the appreciation of women as the 'companions' of men are also very important. We have all heard the term 'family values'. This

Conclusion

new appreciation epitomises that, now, over-used term.

The reformation also succeeded from a political point of view. In many ways, the commoners were extracted out from under the heavy burden of clerical taxation (for example, tithes) at least in Protestant areas. Along with this, the new equality of status let both men and women grasp new opportunities for personal improvement. Moreover, as the reformation (like humanism) tended to focus attention on the worth of the individual, it could certainly be said that a new appreciation for democratic principles allowed the free cities and towns a chance to gain further independence and maintain stability. In other words, from a political perspective, the reformation allowed a certain amount of social levelling. So, clearly, in a number of ways, the reformation could be called successful in fulfilling its objectives. However...

Understanding how the reformation also failed

Basically, each success (above) must be qualified in some way (not least in affecting only Protestant areas) and, almost all of them hide negative aspects.

From a doctrinal point of view this is most clear. Let us review the successes:

- While papal authority was weakened in Protestant areas, it was actually strengthened in Catholic areas and spread further outside Europe.

- While the Mass was changed, Protestants could arrive at no common meaning.

- While the authority of the Bible was recognised, there was no consensus over interpretation (leading, in some cases, into fanaticism).

- While medieval scholastic theology had been undermined, a kind of pseudo-scholasticism developed in its place.

Truly, four unique religious communities had evolved. The problem was that in trying to fortify their own positions they began to view each other as heretics. As a result, the concentration was on spreading their own interpretations (through purpose-built catechisms), surrounding themselves with new and unique theological systems and trying to indoctrinate all believers, rather than on the needs of the believers themselves. This had serious social consequences.

We saw above a number of cultural-social successes. Here again, however, are hidden, negative aspects which must be acknowledged, including:

- the replacement of the Roman clergy's spiritual and political elitism with a new intellectual and social elitism for the pastors
- social equality was recognised, but not really practised.

Because the focus of reform had been the middle, upper and ruling classes, the commoners actually lost ground, remaining ignorant and superstitious and turning back to folklore and magic. Indeed, when Luther refused to support the peasants' war he, in effect, destroyed what might have become a grass-roots social revolution. It consequently became clear to the peasants that the reformers were not really trying to make their lives any better. Indeed, apathy for the reformation more than anything else was the long-term result, for a number of logical reasons:

- Protestant reform depended on literacy
- Catholic priests expected less personal commitment from the laity
- doctrinal changes had no real bearing on the life of the peasant in any real, concrete, way.

It seems to be the case that the reformation did not improve the life of the vast majority. Indeed, with the new emphasis on 'family values', the opportunities for women were actually reduced. Since the religious option was removed (in Protestant areas) women could only be mothers or daughters or wives (other basic patriarchal social norms still applied). Recall too that the position of women in the

Conclusion

Bible was not a particularly good one (from divine after-thought to either temptress or paragon of virtue). Taking this point one step further, seeing the Bible as the only basis of religious truth augmented an already powerful anti-Semitism (especially against Jews, but against Muslims too). Moreover, as the peasants fell back into folklore, the old fear of demons and witches was augmented to drastic levels. Witch hunts became much more prevalent (and frenzied) in Protestant areas. On the Roman Catholic side, from a social perspective, things were not that much better. As censorship was on the rise, art, music and literature became almost as sterile as they became in Calvinist areas.

Lastly, from a political point of view, while the commoners had been relieved of old Roman financial burdens, new taxes were imposed to pay for the new schools, institutions, support of the pastors (and their wives and families!), for printing costs, etc. They were no better and, probably, worse off than before. And while a new appreciation of the individual was, intellectually, formed, the actual reform movement in the urban areas was in the hands of the social elite, and soon degenerated into the pursuit of self-interest. In other words, the town councillors consolidated their own positions by using the reformation as a last-ditch effort for independence (as the towns were in economic decline, they turned to whatever was at hand). Again, the commoners (particularly in rural areas) lost out.

Assessing success and failure depends on your point of view. Yet, clearly, there are today many different Christian religious communities (and they seem to get along) so, despite all the problems, divisions, violence and isolationism, something must have happened to improve things. What happened was a massive war.

The importance of the Thirty Years' War

The one certain consequence of the reformation was the tearing apart of Western Christendom. There can be no denying that the sixteenth century was a time of violent internecine religious conflict (among others), but this religious fervour finally burned itself out as a result of the Thirty Years' War (1618–48).

We will not deal with the war at any length here as religious strife was merely one of many underlying causes (you should read up on it) although it was perhaps the most significant. There are three 'religious' motivations with which the student should be aware:

- several important Catholic rulers, disregarding the Peace of Augsburg, tried to enforce the counter-reformation on the entire Empire
- the Peace of Augsburg had excluded the Calvinists, who were now making serious territorial gains and taking an increasingly anti-Catholic posture
- the Crown of Bohemia had been offered to the Calvinist, Elector Frederick of the Palatinate.

There were, of course, other causes, but religion seems to have been the basis of several of the nastier aspects as each side was advised and counselled by religious figures (particularly the Jesuits) but, of course, politics played a role too.

Understanding the war's impact on religion

By 1648, almost every European nation had experienced some religion-inspired warfare and, quite frankly, people were tired of it. The Treaty of Westphalia had a great many positive results, including:

- the fixture of denominational lines on the European map (at c.1624)
- individual rulers' taking a more relaxed view on their subjects' religious beliefs (the end of 'cuius regio, eius religio')
- the legal recognition of Calvinism
- constitutional guarantees of political representation in the Imperial Diets for all three major religions.

As a further positive result, it came to be regarded as rather naive and backward to mix diplomacy and religion, thus allowing the churches to face interior or philosophical problems as they arose (they even began to co-operate!)

Key Dates

1075	The Investiture Contest established a church free of lay interference.
1215	Fourth Lateran Council reinforced clerical immunity to civil laws.
1302	*Unam Sanctum* (Pope Boniface VIII) declared supreme papal authority.
c.1372	Birth of Jan Hus (Hussite movement)
1377	Church split – two popes each claimed legitimacy.
1415	Jan Hus condemned and burnt.
c.1466	Birth of Erasmus.
1478	Start of Spanish Inquisition.
1480	Birth of Andreas Karlstadt.
1483	Birth of Martin Luther at Eisleben in Saxony.
1484	Birth of Ulrich Zwingli, the Swiss priest and theologian.
1489	Birth of Thomas Müntzer, the radical revolutionary.
1491	Birth of Martin Bucer, the Dominican theologian.
1491	Birth of Ignatius Loyola, founder (with Francis Xavier) of the Jesuits.
1501–2	Luther studied philosophy at Erfurt.
1506	Birth of Francis Xavier, founder (with Loyola) of the Jesuits.
1509	Birth of John Calvin (Jean Chauvin) in Picardy.
1513	Election of Pope Leo X.
1516	Publication of Erasmus's *Greek New Testament*.
1517	Martin Luther publishes his *Ninety-Five Theses* at Wittenberg (October).
1519	Public debate between Martin Luther and Johann Eck.
1520	Martin Luther excommunicated in June.
1518	Elector of Saxony begins to organise a 'Lutheran' church.
1524	Bucer (married in 1522) publishes a statement of reform in Strasbourg.

1525	Thomas Müntzer, the radical revolutionary, tortured and killed.
1525	Battle of Pavia: Emperor Charles V destroyed French army.
1525–26	Peasant revolt in central and southern Germany – 75,000 deaths.
1526	Luther publishes a German service.
1530	The Augsburg Confession – truce between Lutherans and Catholics.
1530	League of Schmalkalden to defend Protestantism.
1531	Death of Zwingli.
1536	Death of Erasmus
1541	Death of Andreas Karlstadt.
1542	Inquisition re-established in Rome.
1545–63	Council of Trent (Catholic counter-reformation).
1551	Death of Martin Bucer.
1555	Augsburg Settlement ended religious war. Future disputes to be settled by law. Principle of *cuius regio, cuius religio* ('who rules, his religion').
1556	Death of Ignatius Loyola, founder of the Jesuits.
1563	Publication of the Heidelberg Catechism claiming legitimacy for the Reformed church.
1564	Death of John Calvin.
1618–48	Thirty Years' War.
1622	Death of Francis Xavier, founder (with Loyola) of the Jesuits.

Glossary

absolution – a formal ecclesiastical release from guilt, liability or punishment.
Anabaptists – radical Protestants who believe that baptism should only be administered to those able to understand and express their faith.
anagogy – prophetic meanings; use of the mundane as reference to the divine.
anti-clericalism – a stance against the power (political, social, economic) of the clergy.
apostolic – relating to the Apostles or the works of the Apostles.
apostolic succession – the transmission of spiritual authority from the Apostles to the popes to the bishops, as claimed by the Roman Catholic church (denied by Protestants).
auricular confession – private confessions heard by a priest.
baptism – a sacrament; the rite of initiation into the church wherein a child is dipped into, or sprinkled with, blessed water.
canonical – in agreement with canon law; authoritative or accepted by the church.
cardinal – a high ecclesiastical administrative rank; also a member of the Sacred College of the Roman church, out of which popes are elected.
catechism – a book, or method, of instruction into the basic tenets of the faith.
celibacy – abstaining from sexual relations.
chrism – consecrated oil sometimes used in the sacrament of baptism or extreme unction.
church – the body of all Christians, laity and clergy; a building the purpose of which is public worship.
conciliarism – a political-philosophical belief that the ecclesiastical authority of the general council is superior to that of the pope.
confirmation – a sacrament; the rite of ratification of baptism.
confraternities – religious groups formed by ordinary laymen.

consecration – a blessing by which some item (object, building) is declared sacred.
consistory – the highest church court or disciplinary body.
consubstantiation – the Lutheran belief that after consecration of the elements, the body and blood co-exist with the bread and wine.
curia – the papal court.
doctrine(s) – a set of beliefs or principles of faith which can be taught.
dogma – a theological principle or tenet of faith sometimes collected together, the truth of which is officially declared by the church.
double predestination – the Calvinist principle which states that God not only 'elected' those predestined for salvation, but also made a positive decision to predestine the 'reprobate' for damnation.
ecumenical – a principle which represents or is agreed by the entire Christian world.
elect – those divinely chosen for salvation.
eucharist – a sacrament; the rite in which the priest offers the dedication, and transforms the bread and wine into the body and blood of Jesus.
evil – morally corrupt or wicked.
extreme unction – a sacrament; the last rite wherein the priest anoints the dying or terminally ill with unction, thereby granting grace.
faith – the firm belief in something without a need for evidence or logical proofs or a system of religious beliefs.
grace – unmerited divine favour; the state in which favour is received.
heresy – any expression, thought or movement judged to be contrary to official church pronouncements on doctrine, dogma or canon law.
Holy Roman Empire – the western European empire established following the coronation of Charlemagne, *c*.800.
Holy Spirit – the third person of the Trinity.
Huguenot – French Protestants of the Calvinist persuasion.
humanism – a system of philosophical thought which is concerned with human achievement or potential rather than with the

Glossary

divine; the cultural movement of the Renaissance which devalued scholasticism in favour of human achievement in the arts and languages and the critical study thereof.

iconoclasm – the breaking or removal of images; the maligning of religious beliefs.

images – visual representations, usually of holy persons (paintings, statues, etc.).

indulgences – papal documents (receipts) issued in exchange for money payments made in lieu of performing a good work.

liturgy – the format of public worship or the set of formularies which prescribe the format.

Mass – the ceremony in which the eucharist is celebrated or the liturgy used in the ceremony.

matrimony – a sacrament; a rite wherein the priest performs the ceremony of marriage while the couple enter into the state of grace for themselves.

mysticism – internalised religious experience; the focus on the hidden or symbolic aspect of faith.

nominalism – a philosophical position wherein general ideas are held to be merely names.

oratory – formal speaking or the art of formal speaking; a small chapel used for private worship.

ordination – a sacrament; the rite by which a man becomes a priest.

Pelagianism – an ancient heresy which claimed that man can influence his own salvation through good works and acts of charity.

penance – a sacrament; the rite by which the individual repents the shame of their sins, including confession, punishment and absolution in the Roman Catholic and Orthodox faiths.

pluralism – the simultaneous holding of more than one ecclesiastical office of benefice.

pope – the head of the Roman Catholic church.

predestination – the religious belief that salvation or damnation was determined by God during the time of creation.

prelate – a senior ecclesiastical officer, usually a bishop, prior or abbot.

priest – an ordained minister of the Roman Catholic, Orthodox or Anglican churches authorised to perform sacramental rites and ceremonies.

Protestant – a descriptive term used to identify a member of any of the western Christian churches apart from the Roman Catholic Church.

proto-Puritanism – the emphasis on religious reform and socio-political change at the grass-roots level at the instigation of the 'common man' for his own benefit, stressing lay preaching and the 'apostolic' religious community; an early form of Puritanism.

purgatory – a place of spiritual cleansing of residual sin through suffering or atonement,

purgation – purification or spiritual cleansing.

puritan – a person practising austere or harsh moral or religious principles.

Puritans – a sect of English Protestants who sought to cleanse the Elizabethan church of unscriptural forms, rites and ceremonies.

real presence – a term used to express the belief in the bodily presence of Jesus in the eucharist.

relic – either some preserved part of the body of a deceased holy person or saint or some preserved material possession of that same person.

religion – the belief in a supernatural controlling power of authority (God or gods) or the expression of this in worship.

religious – the state of devotion to a particular religion; someone who is pious or devout; belonging to a monastic order.

repentance – regret or sorrow for one's previous actions.

reprobate – the damned; those condemned by God; the immoral; those excluded from salvation.

rite – a religious act or ceremony.

sacraments – church ceremonies performed to grant grace to the recipients.

saint – a holy person, declared worthy of veneration by the Roman Catholic or Orthodox church, whose intercession may be publicly sought; the title of such a holy person.

salvation – the act of saving or being saved; ascending to heaven after death.

schism – division into differing or opposing factions owing to disagreements over doctrine.

scholasticism – a method of philosophical or theological speculation

Glossary

aimed at a deeper understanding of religious doctrine and dogma through specialisation, refinement and logical deduction.

schoolman – a practitioner of scholasticism.

scripture – the canonical collection of sacred writings; sometimes replaced by the world 'Bible'.

sin – any act which breaks a divine or moral law; the performance of such an act.

spiritual – the sacred, divine or holy aspect of life.

spiritualism – a philosophical belief that the spirit exists separately from the body; the emphasis on the mystical side of religion.

temporal – the worldly, material or secular aspects of life.

theology – the study of God; the rational or logical analysis of faith, doctrine or dogma; a system of religious principles.

transubstantiation – the Roman Catholic belief that the bread and wine are transformed into the body and blood of Jesus in the eucharist.

tropology – moral, ethical or figurative meanings.

vernacular – the language or dialect of a particular country, region or group.

Vulgate – the Latin version of the Bible accepted as canonical by the Roman Catholic church.

Sources

The following is a list of sources used and of further recommended readings in English.

Introduction

E Cameron, *The European Reformation* (Oxford, 1991)
O Chadwick, *The Reformation* (Harmondsworth, 1964)
A G Dickens & J Tonkin, *The Reformation in Historical Thought* (Oxford, 1985)
G R Elton, *Reformation Europe 1517–1559* (London, 1963)
M Greengrass, *The Longman Companion to the European Reformation c.1500–1618* (London, 1998)
H J Hillerbrand, *The World of the Reformation* (London, 1973)
H J Hillerbrand (ed.), *The Protestant Reformation* (New York, 1968)
M Hughes, *Early Modern Germany, 1477–1806* (London, 1992)
R Mackenny, *Sixteenth Century Europe: Expansion and Conflict* (London, 1993)
A McGrath, *Reformation Thought* (Oxford, 1988)
B M G Reardon, *Religious Thought in the Reformation* (London, 1981)
A Johnston, *The Protestant Reformation in Europe* (London, 1991)
C Lindberg, *The European Reformations* (Oxford, 1996)

Chapter 1

C Augustijn, *Erasmus: His Life, Works, and Influence*, trans. by J C Grayson (Toronto, 1991)
R Bainton, *Erasmus* (Tring, 1969)
A G Dickens & W R D Jones, *Erasmus the Reformer* (London, 1994)
V H H Green, *Renaissance and Reformation* (London, 1952)
A Goodman & A Mackay (eds), *The Impact of Humanism on Western Europe* (London, 1990)
P O Kristeller, *Renaissance Thought* (London, 1961)
H A Oberman, *The Harvest of Medieval Theology* (Durham, N.C., 1983)

Chapter 2
S L Greenslade (ed.), *The Cambridge History of the Bible: The West from the Reformation to the Present Day* (Cambridge, 1963)
D Englander *et al.* (eds), *Culture and Belief in Europe 1450–1600: An Anthology of Sources* (Oxford, 1990)
H Kamen, *European Society, 1500–1700* (London, 1992 edn)
A McGrath, *The Intellectual Origins of the European Reformation* (Oxford, 1987)
A McGrath, *Christian Theology: An Introduction* (Oxford, 1994)

Chapter 3
Luther's Works (55 vols., St Louis, 1955–75)
J Dillenberger (ed.), *Martin Luther: Selections from his Writings* (New York, 1961)
E G Rupp and B Drewery (eds.), *Martin Luther: Documents of Modern History* (London, 1970)
K Randell, *Luther and the German Reformation* (Sevenoaks, 1989)
R Bainton, *Here I Stand: Martin Luther* (Oxford, 1978)
J Atkinson, *Martin Luther and the Birth of Protestantism* (Harmondsworth, 1968)
P N Brooks (ed.), *Seven-Headed Luther* (Oxford, 1983)
V H H Green, *Luther and the Reformation* (London, 1964)
B Lohse, *Martin Luther: An Introduction to his Life and Thought* (Edinburgh, 1987)

Chapter 4
L J Abray, *The People's Reformation: Magistrates, Clergy, and Commons in Strasbourg 1500–1598* (Oxford, 1985)
T A Brady, *Turning Swiss: Cities and Empire, 1450–1550* (Cambridge, 1985)
G Potter, *Ulrich Zwingli* (London, 1977)
W P Stephens, *Zwingli: An Introduction to his Thought* (Oxford, 1993)
N Birnbaum, 'The Zwinglian Reformation in Zurich', in *Past and Present 15* (1959), pp.27–47
S E Ozment, *The Reformation in the Cities* (New Haven, Conn., 1975)
W P Stephens, *The Theology of Huldrych Zwingli* (Oxford, 1986)
W P Stephens, *The Holy Spirit in the Theology of Martin Bucer* (Cambridge, 1970)

D R Wright (ed.), *Common Places of Martin Bucer* (Abingdon, 1972)

Chapter 5
P Blickle, *The Revolution of 1525: The German Peasants' War from a New Perspective*, trans. by T A Brady and H C Erik Midelfort (Baltimore, 1981)

E W Gritsch, 'Thomas Müntzer and Luther: A Tragedy of Errors', in H J Hillerbrand (ed.), *Radical Tendencies in the Reformation* (Kirksville, MO., 1988), pp.55–84

J M Stayer, 'Christianity in One City: Anabaptist Münster, 1534–35' in H J Hillerbrand (ed.), *Radical Tendencies in the Reformation* (Kirksville, MO., 1988), pp.117–34

C-P Clasen, *Anabaptism. A Social History 1525–1618* (London, 1972)

M Stayer, *Anabaptism and the Sword* (Lawrence, 1976 2nd ed.)

Chapter 6
S Looß, 'Radical views of the early Andreas Karlstadt (1520-25)', in H J Hillerbrand (ed.), *Radical Tendencies in the Reformation* (Kirksville, MO., 1988), pp.43–54

G Rupp, 'Andrew Karlstadt and the Reformation Puritanism', in *Journal of Theological Studies n.s. 10* (1959), pp.308–26

H J Hillerbrand, 'Andreas Bodenstein of Carlstadt', in *Church History 35* (1966), pp.379–98

R J Sider, *Andreas Bodenstein von Karlstadt, The Development of his Thought 1517–1525* (Leyden, 1974)

H Guggisberg, *Basel in the Sixteenth Century* (St Louis, 1982)

Chapter 7
B Hall, *John Calvin* (London, 1956)

H Höpfl (ed.), *Luther and Calvin on Secular Authority* (Cambridge, 1991)

M Mullet, *Calvin* (London, 1989)

A McGrath, *A Life of John Calvin* (Oxford, 1990)

J C Olin (ed.), *Calvin and Sadoleto: A Reformation Debate* (New York, 1966)

K Randell, *Calvin and the Later Reformation* (London, 1988)

F Wendel, *Calvin* (London, 1980)

R S Wallace, *Calvin, Geneva and the Reformation* (Edinburgh, 1988)

A Duke, G Lewis & A Pettegree (eds), *Calvinism in Europe 1540-1610,*

A Collection of Documents (Manchester, 1992)

Chapter 8
N S Davidson, *The Counter-Reformation* (Oxford, 1987)
B J Kidd, *The Counter-Reformation, 1550–1600* (London, 1933)
S J Lee, *Aspects of European History 1494–1789* (London, 1992)
M Mullet, *The Counter-Reformation* (London, 1984)
K Randell, *The Catholic and Counter-Reformation* (London, 1990)
A G Dickens, *The Counter Reformation* (New York, 1979)
H Jedin, *A History of the Council of Trent 2 vols.* (London, 1957–61)
L Châtellier, *The Europe of the Devout* (Cambridge, 1987)
J O'Malley, *The First Jesuits* (Cambridge, Mass., 1993)
W V Bangert, *A History of the Society of Jesus* (St Louis, 1986 2nd ed.)

Conclusion
G Benicke, *Germany in the Thirty Years' War: Documents of Modern History* (London, 1978)
G Parker (ed.), *The Thirty Years' War* (London, 1991 edn.)

Web Sites for Reformation Studies

The internet, or world wide web, is an amazingly useful resource, giving the history student nearly free and almost immediate information on any topic. Ignore this vast and valuable store of materials at your peril! The following list of web sites may be helpful for your further readings on:

- primary documents – like books
- secondary sources – like academic papers
- visual aids – like maps, buildings, portraits.

Note – Neither the author nor the publisher is responsible for content or opinions expressed on the sites listed, which are simply intended to offer starting points for students exploring Reformation Studies. Also, please remember that the internet is a fast-evolving environment, and links may come and go. If you have some favourite sites you would like to see mentioned in future editions of this book, please write to Dr Andrew Chibi, c/o Studymates (address on back cover). You will find a free selection of useful and ready-made student links for history and other subjects at the Studymates web site:

http://www.studymates.co.uk

Happy surfing!

The Protestant reformation in general
Calvin and Luther
http://history.hanover.edu/early/prot.htm

Web Sites for Reformation Studies

These pages provide a good collection of primary sources, including readily available translations of the writings of Calvin and Luther.

Resource materials
http://www.remembrancer.com/ink/default.htm
Here is another good site with resource materials, providing many difficult to find primary sources and other related documents.

Index of related web sites
http://www.educ.msu.edu/homepages/laurence/reformation/index.htm
An online index of related web sites, including links to people, materials and related institutions in Europe and America.

Reformation and Counter-Reformation
http://www.johnco.cc.ks.us/~jjackson/refo.html
The site offers an online discussion paper on the reformation and counter-reformation.

Historical materials and links
http://services.csi.it/~valdese/english.htm
Here is a unique site tracing historical materials from Valdo of Lyon to the present Waldensian Church of Turin, Italy. These pages offer much variety, potential for exploration, and good reformation links.

Reformation & Counter-Reformation
http://www.stedwards.edu/cfpages/stoll/iw/reformtn.htm
These pages provide a detailed and varied exploration of ancient to modern history with an extremely impressive early modern section, papal and church history, several reformation links (both Protestant and Catholic) plus several important documents and related web sites available for your reference.

The Catholic Reformation
http://www.ewtn.com/library/homelibr/ropscare.txt
This site is a very readable essay on several aspects of reformation history by Henri Daniel-Rops.

Martin Luther

What was the Lutheran Reformation?
http://www.ultranet.com/~tlclcms/whatwas.htm
A short, but useful online discussion paper by Richard Bucher, Pastor.

Luther sources in translation
http://www.mun.ca/rels/hrollmann/reform/reform.html
These well-indexed pages by Dr Hans Rollmann provide a number of primary Luther sources in translation, as well as other related documents (*Hymnals, The Augsburg Confession*, and others).

Treasures of Saxon State Library
http://www.loc.gov/exhibits/dres/dres3.html
These pages deal with the ramifications of Luther in Saxony and Germany specifically and provide useful information on particular Luther-related events such as the indulgence crisis.

Colour portrait of Luther
http://www.research.ibm.com/image_apps/luthp.html
This page provides the famous colour portrait of Luther from the Boston College archives along with a number of related applications.

Selected writings
http://www.bc.edu/bc_org/avp/cas/ger/luther.html
An online reference guide to about 323 selected writings for scholarly use. An electronically accessible *Index Verborum*, drawn from a critical decade of Dr Martin Luther's writings from the period 1516–1525, is being created in the Department of German Studies at Boston College in Massachusetts, USA. Here are links to the Project Luther web site.

Project Wittenberg
http://www.iclnet.org/pub/resources/text/wittenberg/wittenberg-home.html
These pages (on a massive site) provide a link to the Project Wittenberg homepage, which links to several other related sites of Luther and Lutheran materials, including people, works and

images, church statements, and modern materials.

Saxon State Library Exhibit
http://lcweb.loc.gov/exhibits/dres/dres3.html
These pages provide an interesting online tour of the 'Reformation in Germany (Saxon State Library Exhibit)', including treasures, books, manuscripts, paintings. A good visual aid.

Luther's 'Dedication to the Christian Reader'
http://www.iclnet.org/pub/resources/text/wittenberg/luther/luther-reader.txt
This page provides a good translation of Luther's *Dedication to the Christian Reader* of 1545.

Small Catechism and Large Catechism
http://www.iclnet.org/pub/resources/text/wittenberg/wittenberg-luther.html
These clearly indexed pages provide many useful selections and a link to the Project Wittenberg sites. Selections from the *Small Catechism* (1529) and the *Large Catechism* (1530) are included.

Translations
http://www.iclnet.org/pub/resources/text/wittenberg/wittenberg-boc.html
These pages provide useful translations of the *Treatise of the Power and Primacy of the Pope* (1537) and *The Augsburg Confession* (1530).

Treatise on Good Works
http://www.iclnet.org/pub/resources/text/wittenberg/wittenberg-luthworks.html
This page provides a good translation of Luther's *A Treatise on Good Works* (1520).

The Ninety-Five Theses (Latin)
http://www.iclnet.org/pub/resources/text/wittenberg/luther/ninetyfive-latin.txt
This page provides the Latin text of the *Ninety-Five Theses*.

The Ninety-Five Theses (English)
http://www.iclnet.org/pub/resources/text/wittenberg/luther/ninetyfive.txt
This page provides a good English translation of the *Ninety-Five Theses*.

Luther on indulgences
http://www.iclnet.org/pub/resources/text/wittenberg/luther/nine5-albrecht.txt
http://www.fordham.edu/halsall/source/lutherltr-indulgences.html
These pages provides good translations of Luther's *Letter to the Archbishop Albrecht of Mainz* regarding indulgences.

Luther's Letter to Pope Leo X
http://www.iclnet.org/pub/resources/text/wittenberg/luther/nine5-pope.txt
This page provides a good translation of Luther's *Letter to Pope Leo X* which accompanied the *Resolutions to the XCV Theses* (1518).

Luther's Letter to John Staupitz
http://www.iclnet.org/pub/resources/text/wittenberg/luther/nine5-staupitz.txt
This page provides a good translation of Luther's *Letter to John Staupitz* which accompanied the *Resolutions to the XCX Theses* (1518).

Visual Lutheran resources
http://rmc-www.library.cornell.edu/paper-exhibit/luther.html
Here is an impressive site for visual resources. There are several pages showing pictures of Luther's Bible, other Bibles, and a table of contents to other sites on Bible translation history and other useful topics.

Luther's Die Bibel
http://www.hti.umich.edu/relig/luther
This is another impressive site, whose pages provide search engines of words and phrases from Luther's *Die Bibel* translation, as well as a general browse tool.

Web Sites for Reformation Studies

Die Bibel
http://nobi.ethz.ch/bibel/buecher.html
These pages (in German) provide the hypertext version of Luther's *Die Bibel*.

Luther's Preface to the Letter of St Paul to the Romans.
http://ccel.wheaton.edu/luther/romans/pref_romans.html
This page provides a useful translation of Luther's *Preface to the Letter of St Paul to the Romans*.

John Calvin
Calvin Institute for Theology
http://capo.org/calvin/ccalvin.html
This is the web site of the Calvin Institute for Theology. It offers useful links to reformation studies sites, Calvin's writings, Erasmus, Bible studies and several modern connections. Highly recommended.

Christian Classics Ethereal Library
http://ccel.wheaton.edu/calvin/christian_life/christian_life.html
http://ccel.wheaton.edu/calvin/prayer/prayer.html
http://ccel.wheaton.edu/calvin/commentaries/commentaries.html
These pages link to the Christian Classics Ethereal Library, which offers a number of primary sources in translation, for example Calvin's *On The Christian Life, Of Prayer*, and his *Commentaries* among several others.

Calvin's Institutes
http://www.smartlink.net/~douglas/calvin/entire.html
These pages provide a nice copy of Calvin's *Institutes*, a most useful resource.

National Protestant Church of Geneva
http://wccx.wcc-coe.org/enpg/welc_eng.html
This is the web site of the National Protestant Church of Geneva, offering (in French or English option) an exploration of historical developments. An interesting and educational tool.

Medieval Source
http://www.fordham.edu/halsall/source/calvin-onclergy.html
This web site offers Calvin's *Letter to the King* [On the Clergy] in translation. It also provides a link to the Medieval Source site [www.fordham.edu/halsall/sbook.html] which explores many medieval to modern historical events. Note: the student is directed towards www.fordham.edu/halsall/sbooklx.html which deals with the Renaissance (sources, books, biographies, artists, politics and humanism), or towards www.fordham.edu/halsall/sbookly which deals extensively with similar reformation materials.

Canons of Dort
http://www.reformed.org/documents/synod_of_dort.html
http://www.geocities.com/Heartland/1136/cod.htm
These two sites provide an online text (in translation) of the important statement of faith, the *Canons of Dort* (1619).

Essay on Presbyterianism
http://www.reformed.org/calvinism/5Points_Dabney.html
This is a very long online essay on Presbyterianism and its relations to Calvinism, written by R L Dabney (*c*.1864). The site contains a link to the CRTA (Center for Reformed Theology Apologetics) homepage, which is well worth exploring.

A defence of Calvinism
http://www.reformed.org/calvinism/Spurgeon-Calvinism.html
An interesting, if brief, online article exploring a defence of Calvinism, written by C H Spurgeon, and containing a link to the CRTA homepage.

Calvinist doctrine
http://reformed.org/calvinism/calvinism.html
This is a basic web site outlining the major aspects of Calvinist doctrine. It provides links to several other online articles on different aspects, including doctrine, people and related religious like Puritanism or Arminianism.

Web Sites for Reformation Studies

Ulrich Zwingli

Life of Ulrich Zwingli
http://www.csn.net/advent/cathen/15772a.htm
These pages provide a useful online resource detailing the career of Ulrich Zwingli. Included in the paper are modern associations, a discussion of contemporaries and a discussion of primary resources.

Church History Institute
http://www1.gospelcom.net/chi/glimpses/sixteen.html
This is the site of the Church History Institute. It offers a good discussion paper on the impact on Zurich of Zwingli's reform movement, incorporating pictures and text.

Views on the Lord's Supper
http://silcon.com/~akraus/ecumenism/lordsupr.html
You will find a useful discussion of Zwingli's views on the Lord's Supper, compared with those of Martin Luther. It explores the arguments in full, including sources and good reference materials.

Radical reformation

Radical sects of the reformation
http://www.cc.ukans.edu/~hisite/gilbert/15
This site provides quite a detailed description of the radical sects of the reformation, the Anabaptists in particular. A very useful resource.

Anabaptists
http://www.goshen.net/~critch/libraryofgod/anabaps.html
This is a large site, providing useful information on the Anabaptists. The article details teachings, social and religious impact, reactions, and also provides a useful bibliography and historiographical discussion.

Christianity Today: Menno Simons
http://www.christianity.net/ct/6TB/6TB044.html
A large site taken from the files of the *Christianity Today* journal. Menno Simons is the subject. These pages provide useful insights

into this important historical figure and makes useful comparisons to modern-day cult figures.

Modern repercussions
http://www.goshen.edu/~paulmr/Menno.html
Mennonite-related information on the internet – a site of internet links. It is particularly useful for tracing modern repercussions from radical reformation beginnings.

Translations of primary materials
http://www.geocities.com/Heartland/1136.html
This unstable site provides useful translations of primary materials, like the Heidelberg Catechism or the Belgic Confession of Faith, but only when it is up and running.

Catholic/counter-reformation
Primary documents and texts
http://history.hanover.edu/early/cath.htm
These pages from Hanover College, USA, contain a useful selection of primary documents, hard-to-find texts, and other resources in translation.

Loyola's Spiritual Exercises
http://www.fordham.edu/halsall/source/loyola-spirex.html
This page provides a useful translation of the most important aspects of St Ignatius Loyola's *Spiritual Exercises*, the rules of the Jesuit order.

The Council of Trent
http://history.hanover.edu/early/trent.htm
In time, this site will feature the full text of the canons of the Council of Trent, a session-by-session examination, and the decrees, and will have links to other sites.

Protestant and Catholic reformations
http://history.hanover.edu/europe.htm
This is highly recommended. The site contains materials on early modern history, particularly useful on the Protestant and Catholic reformations. It offers several resources.

St John of the Cross
http://ccel.wheaton.edu/john_of_the_cross/ascent/ascent.html
http://ccel.wheaton.edu/john_of_the_cross/dark_night/dark_night.html
http://ccel.wheaton.edu/john_of_the_cross/canticle/canticle.html
These are resource pages devoted to the writings of St John of the Cross (1542–1591), featuring his *The Ascent of Mt.Carmel, Dark Night of the Soul, A Spiritual Canticle of the Soul* and the *Bridegroom of Christ*. Very readable material.

Teresa of Avila
http://ccel.wheaton.edu/teresa/way/main.html
http://ccel.wheaton.edu/teresa/life/main.html
http://ccel.wheaton.edu/teresa/castle/castle.html
These are resource pages devoted to the the writings of Teresa of Avila (1516–1582), featuring her *The Way of Perfection, Interior Castle*, and a biography *The Life of St Teresa of Jesus*. It offers a number of useful starting points.

European Reformation Syllabuses

Universities with Early Modern Europe core modules (a sampling)
Bristol	Kent
Brunel	Liverpool
Dundee	Newcastle
Edinburgh	Northumbria
Exeter	Reading
Glasgow	Sheffield
Hertfordshire	Southampton
Hull	Wolverhampton
Keele	

Universities with reformation-related projects
St Andrews Institute of Reformation Studies
Centre for Reformation Studies (Sheffield)
Leicester University Centre for Religious Studies

Example university course offerings
Aberdeen	Themes and Variations: Europe and Scotland, 1500–1750
Bangor	The Birth of Modern Europe
	The Reformation and Counter Reformation in Europe
Buckingham	Church and Society, 1400–1900
De Montfort	Division and Disorder in the 16th Century
Durham (History)	State and Society in Early Modern Europe, 1500–1715
	The Papacy, 1379–1520
	Society and Culture in the Low Countries, 1477–1688
	The Catholic Renewal in Europe, 1540–1620
Durham (Theology)	The Early Church and the Reformation

European Reformation Syllabuses

	Christ and Salvation: the Early Church and the Reformation
	Theology and History of the Reformation & Counter Reformation
Essex	The Making of Early Modern Europe, 1500–1770
Goldsmiths (UL)	Reform and Renewal: Religious Life in Britain and Europe in the Age of Reformation and Counter Reformation
Huddersfield	Reformation and Revolution: Britain 1485–1660
Lancaster	The Origins of Modern Europe from Luther's Reformation to the French Revolution, 1517–1713
Leicester	Erasmus, Machiavelli and More: Writers in an Age of Crisis
Kings (UL)	European History, 1500–1800 (main papers)
	(Themes) in Early Modern Cultural History
Manchester Metro.	Politics and Society in Western Europe
	Politics and Society in Western Europe (p/t Adult)
Middlesex	The Origins of Modern Europe c.1400–1600
	The Reformation and Social Conflict
Nottingham Trent	Traditions and Transformations: Europe 1000–1600
Portsmouth	Popular Culture and Popular Rebellion in Europe c.1380–1530
Sheffield	The European Reformation
Sheffield (Adult)	The Reformation: Reaction and Action, 1517–1688
Southampton	Government in Western Europe
Strathclyde	Europe in the Renaissance and Reformation
Sunderland	Foundations of Modern Europe
Swansea	The Church in Late Medieval Europe
Warwick	Germany in the Age of Reform
West of England	Themes in Early Modern Europe, 1480–1780
	The Holy Roman Empire in the Confessional

York Age: Religion, Society and Politics in Germany, 1517–1648
Resistance and Reformation: Challenges to Authority in Europe, 1250–1550
Church, State and Society, 1550–1750

Northern Examinations and Assessment Board (1999)

Religious Studies Syllabus: Alternative D – Aspects of the History of the Christian Church (section 1)

(b) Catholic reformation aspects
(c) Protestant reformation aspects

History Syllabus: Alternative B – Europe in Transition

1. The new learning and religious controversy in sixteenth-century Europe
2. Authority and the State

History Syllabus: Alternative J – Britain, 1485–1603

1. The crisis of the Tudor State, 1547–58
2. Stability and reformation, 1485–1547
3. The age of Elizabeth, 1558–1603

Southern (AEB) (1999)

History Syllabus 0630: Period Studies (Option 01) English and/or European History, 1450–1760

Part I (1450–1559) – Section C: Economic, social and cultural history
Part II (1559–1660) – Section C: Economic, social and cultural history

European Reformation Syllabuses

London Examinations GCE (Advanced)
Religious Studies Syllabus: Advanced

   Unit C Christianity and the Christian Church
   Section 3: The Reformation Period (a and c)

Religious Studies Syllabus: Advanced Supplementary

   Unit C: Christianity and the Christian Church
   Section 3: The Reformation Period (a and c)

History Syllabus: Advanced

   Syllabus A Paper 12: European History, 1516–1815
            The Protestant Reformation of the Sixteenth Century
            The Catholic Reformation
            The Thirty Years War

   Syllabus B Paper 2: The Reformation in Europe, 1517–1563

Index

à Kempis, Thomas, 17
absenteeism, 27
absolution, 32, 44
Albrecht of Brandenburg, 40
allegory, 62
Allstadt, 73, 83
Amish, 67
Anabaptists (-ism), 62, 67–75
anagogy, 62
anti-clericalism, 15, 17, 23
anti-papalism, 15, 17, 22–3
Aquinas, Thomas, 20
Augsburg, 41
   confession, 52
   peace of, 116
   settlement, 52
Augustinians, 40–1, 105
Avignon, 17

Basel, 55, 58, 85
Berne, 68
Bible, the, 32, 37, 46–7, (Karlstadt on) 78, (Luther on) 78–9
   New Testament, 10
   Old Testament, 34
bishops, 26–7, (duties of), 108
Black Death, the, 15, 56
Bohemia, 22, 35
Bologna, Concordat of, 26
Brockelson, Jan, 74
Brooks, Mel, 103
Bucer, Martin, 55, 57–9 (on justification) 61, (on the Eucharist), 63

Cajetan (Tomas de Vio), 40–1, 46, 99
Calvin (-ism, -ist), 9, 69, 74, 83–96,
   on church/state, 93–4
   on Church visible/invisible, 92–5
   on double predestination 87–9, 95

on free will 88–9
(on Jesus) 90–1
on salvation, 88–91, 95
on the sacraments, 91–2, 95
Capuchins, 98–9 on double
Catechism,
   Large, 48
   Small, 48
Catholic reformation, 9, 97–110
Charles V, 101, 105
Church,
   and state, 64–5, 70, 80
   'visible/invisible', 64, 69, 92–4, 95
Cologne, 40
conciliarism, 16–8, 23
confession, 32, 44
confraternities, 26
Constance, 17
Constitutions, the, 100
consubstantiation, 46
Contarini, Gasparo, 102
contrition, 32
Counter reformation, 9, 11, 97–110
cuius regio, euis religio, 52, 86, 93, 116
curia, the papal, 26, 56

d'Etaples, 21
Dickens, A G, 55
Donation of Constantine, 16

Eck, Johann, 40–1, 76
England, 22, 35, 94
Erasmus, 21–3, 57, 59
   on free will, 89, 98, 102

faith, 50, 60
Florence, 97
France, 11, 21, 55, 101
Francis I, 26, 94, 101, 105
Frederick (the Wise), 73

Index

Geneva, 85, 94
Germany, 39, 52
good works, 19
grace, 28–30
Greek New Testament, 22, 34, 57, 98

Heidelberg, 58
   Catechism, 87
heresy, 37
Hoffman, Melchior, 73
Holy Roman Empire, 15, 30
Huguenot(s), 94
humanism (-ists, -ist), 15, 20, 23, 34
   Christian, 21
   civic, 21
Hungary, 94
Hus, Jan, 35
Hussites, 22, 35

iconoclasm, 80
Index, the, 102–3, 109
indulgence(s), 18–19, 31, 36, 38
Inquisition, the, 10, 103–4, 109
Institutions of the Christian religion, 85
Investiture contest, 16
Italy, 13, 15, 21, 23, 56

Jerome, St, 33
Jerusalem, 30
Jesuits, 98, 100–1, 109
Jesus, 14, 19, 28, 47, 53, 58, 60, 65, 73–4,
   Karlstadt on, 78–9
   Zwingli on, 60
justification, 28–9
   double, 61, 65

Karlstadt, Andreas, 76–84
   on baptism, 81–2
   Peasants' Revolt, 82–3

Lateran Council, 16
Leipzig, 41
liturgy, 32–3
Lollards (-y), 22, 35
Loyola, Ignatius, 98, 100
Luther (-an, -ism), 9, 23, 35, 38-54, 58–60, 72, 76–7

Machiavelli, 22–3

Mainz, 40
Mass, the, 18, 35, 43 46, 59
Melchiorites, 73
Mennonites, 67
Mongols, the, 15
Monty Python and th Holy Grail, 78, 103
Münster, 67, 73–4
Müntzer, Thomas, 67, 72–3, 83

Netherlands, the, 74, 94
Ninety-Five Theses, 38
nominalism, 20, 30, 35

Oecolampadius, 55, 57–9
   on justification, 61
Oratories, 98–9
original sin, 14, 29, 49–50, 60, 107

Palestine, 100
Paris, 34
Pavia, 101
Peasants' revo t, 52, 73
Pelagianism, 29–30, 36, 70, 77
Philip (the Fair), 17
piety, 18, 22–3, 82
Pisa, 17
pluralism, 27
Poland, 94
pope (papal, papacy), 10, 16, 22, 25–6, 30, 41–2, 44–5
   authority, 107
   reform 101–2
   Adrian VI, 101
   Boniface VIII, 17
   Clement V, 17
   Clement VII, 101
   Innocent III, 16
   Leo X, 26, 40
   Martin V, 17–8
   Paul III, 101–2, 105
   Paul IV, 99, 102
   Urban II, 16
predestination, 28, 50, 61, 77
priesthood of all believers, 43–5, 48–9, 53, 56, 64
priests duties, 108
proto-Puritanism, 76–8, 83
purgatory, 18–20, 28–31, 36, 39, 42–3, 57

Quakers, 67

Radical (-s, -ism), 9, 11, 67–75
real presence, 45–6, 53, 62–3, 91
realism, 20, 30
Reformation, 9, 10, 25, 111–5
   magisterial, 11
   mainstream, 11
   Protestant, 11
   urban, 11, 55–66
Reformed religion, 9, 85–96
regeneration, 32, 50, 78
Renaissance, the, 13, 14–16, 23
repentance, 50
Reply to Sadoleto, 85
Rothenburg, 82
Rothmann, Bernard, 73

Sacraments, the seven, 31–2, 37, 43, 107
   Baptism, 31, 45, 48, 53
      radicals, 69–71
      three-fold, 74–5, 91
   confirmation, 31
   eucharist, 31, 45, 53
      Karlstadt on, 79–80, 83, 91, 95
      Lord's Supper, 74
   extreme unction, 31
   matrimony, 31
   ordination, 31, 44, 48
   penance, 20, 31, 44
St Gallen, 68
St Peter's, 40
salvation, 49–50, 59–61, 77
satisfaction, 32
Savonarola, 97
Schmalkalden, league of, 52
schola Augustiniana, 20
scholasticism, 14, 20–1, 32, 77
schoolman, 14, 33
Scotland, 94
Scotus, Duns, 106
sola experientia, 67, 71–2, 74
sola fideism, 43, 47, 51–3, 56–7, 60–1, 72
   Zwingli on, 61
sola scriptura, 42, 46–7, 53, 67, 70

Spain, 21, 56, 97
Spiritual Exercises, the, 100
Spiritualism, 67, 71–2, 83
Strasbourg, 55–6, 58, 73, 85, 93
Switzerland, 11, 55, 58, 94

Tetzel, Johann, 39–40
Theatines, 99
Thirty Years' War, the, 115–6
Thomists, 106
transubstantiation, 31, 45, 63
Trent, Council of, 18, 102, 104–9
   administrative reforms, 108–9
   doctrinal authority, 106
   on salvation, 106
   sola fideism, 106
   the *Vulgate*, 106
Trier, 40
Trinity, doctrine of the, 14
troplogy, 62

Unam Sanctum, 17
Ursulines, 99

Valdes, Peter, 35
via moderna, 20
Vulgate, 22, 33

Waldenses, 22, 35–6
Wartburg, 79
Western Schism, the, 16–8, 23
Westphalia, peace of, 116
William of Ockham, 20
Wittenberg, 38–9, 76
   disturbances, 79
Wyclif, John, 35

Xavier, Francis, 100
Ximenes, 21

Zürich, 55, 58, 64–5, 68
Zwickau, 72
Zwingli, Uldrich, 55, 57–9
   infant baptism, 62–3, 65
   justification, 61
   scripture, 62, 64
   the Eucharist, 63, 65